Mary Hunter Austin
A Female Writer's Protest Against the First World War in the United States

Jowan A. Mohammed
Nord University, Norway

Series in American History

Copyright © 2022 Vernon Press, an imprint of Vernon Art and Science Inc, on behalf of the author.

All rights reserved. No part of this publication may be reproduced, stored in a retrieval system, or transmitted in any form or by any means, electronic, mechanical, photocopying, recording, or otherwise, without the prior permission of Vernon Art and Science Inc.

www.vernonpress.com

In the Americas:
Vernon Press
1000 N West Street, Suite 1200
Wilmington, Delaware, 19801
United States

In the rest of the world:
Vernon Press
C/Sancti Espiritu 17,
Malaga, 29006
Spain

Series in American History

Library of Congress Control Number: 2021938622

ISBN: 978-1-64889-357-5

Also available: 978-1-62273-753-6 [Hardback]; 978-1-64889-319-3 [PDF, E-Book]

Cover design by Vernon Press using elements designed by rawpixel.com / Freepik.

Product and company names mentioned in this work are the trademarks of their respective owners. While every care has been taken in preparing this work, neither the authors nor Vernon Art and Science Inc. may be held responsible for any loss or damage caused or alleged to be caused directly or indirectly by the information contained in it.

Every effort has been made to trace all copyright holders, but if any have been inadvertently overlooked the publisher will be pleased to include any necessary credits in any subsequent reprint or edition.

To my parents.

Table of contents

	Preface	*vii*
	Introduction	*xi*
Chapter 1	**Mary Hunter Austin (1868-1934): Life and Works**	1
Chapter 2	**The Impact of World War One**	35
Chapter 3	**Mary Hunter Austin's Writings (1917-1920)**	57
	The Ford (1917)	
	The Young Woman Citizen (1918)	
	"Sex Emancipation Through War" (1918)	
	No. 26 Jayne Street (1920)	
Chapter 4	**Later Perceptions of Austin's Works**	97
	Conclusion	*125*
	Works Cited	*129*
	Index	*139*

Preface

The way we tend to read and interpret the past is very much related to our understanding of the present. Societies redefine their own history and decide about the historiographical focus upon the latter. While historians—that, for a long period of time, meant men—defined the past by taking a look at the lives of the "great men of the past." Thereby a male monopoly of history was created, often only caring to cement the inequalities of an existent society that was much more diverse than history books would actually acknowledge. Thankfully, we live in a time period where minorities, may they be determined by ethnicity, social status, or gender, are taken more into consideration when we discuss the human past.

Nevertheless, women's impact on history still needs to be discovered, identified, spread to become public knowledge, and eventually acknowledged by a majority of people. Women fought for their rights for centuries, but many brave minds still remain underrepresented and less appreciated in our days, although feminist movements already pointed to these figures in earlier years as well. The danger to forget them is again very high, and more works on issues related to gender and women's history should be encouraged at universities worldwide.

Mary Hunter Austin (1868-1934) was such an essential mind related to gender and women's history. Very often, however, she is just referred to as a female writer of the American Midwest, whose works provide important descriptions of the landscape and the people in this part of the United States at the end of the 19th and the beginning of the 20th century. Yet Hunter Austin was more than that. She was a woman that no longer accepted the boundaries of a society that had been hegemonically ruled and determined by men. The young woman rebelled against the world she was born into, and demanded a better future for herself and all women alike. Especially during the First World War (1914-1918), Hunter Austin, like many other American women, was active to achieve more rights, particularly citizenship rights, for women and protested against old-fashioned gender roles.

The enslavement and exploitation of the female body and mind by an antiquated society were not acceptable to a woman whose personal life had been shaped by arrogant men, who did not grant her equality in any sense.

It is the great merit of Jowan A. Mohammed to again critically review the life and achievements of such an important woman and her history during the transnational event US diplomat and historian George F. Kennan (1904-2005) referred to as the "seminal catastrophe" of the 20th century. The present study is an interdisciplinary approach to show how Hunter Austin's life was impacted by this war and how it stimulated her attempt to help to gain more rights for women. They, according to the female activist, had also proven more than worthy to be recognized as equal citizens of the United States. The study therefore combines and addresses different fields of study, namely military history, gender studies, and modern American literature. A close reading of Austin's literary works in the years related to the First World War shows how the "proto-feminist" author's political agenda was interwoven with her personal experiences and the war-related activism, especially in New York City at that time, alike.

The present book consequently proves to be valuable for different readers. Those who are interested in the history of New York will be able to dive into a radical female milieu that existed in this US metropolis during the First World War. Those readers whose field of interest is women's and gender history will find an analysis of problems that women born in the second half of the 19th century had to face in the United States; furthermore, a scientific discussion of female responses to this situation—represented by Mary Hunter Austin in the present study. Finally, readers looking for an analysis of unknown works of modern American literature, whose author was rediscovered during the American feminist movement in the latter half of the 20th century, will find an equally close reading.

The present book is, therefore, the result of an interdisciplinary approach and not only a simple biographical study. It is obviously much more than that. It is the attempt to re-evaluate the role of a strong woman in modern American history, to view her story, and to read her works from a different angle, no longer solely focusing on landscapes and the people of the Midwest. Jowan A. Mohammed provides a splendid and tremendously important work that will hopefully stimulate further research that will follow this direction, as there were many strong women in all parts of the United States—and other countries as well—whose fight for freedom, equality, and justice needs to be taken into further consideration. This is even more important in times when gender equality is again threatened by political reactionism.

True equality can only be achieved if the merits and achievements of women and men are accepted equally by society. To reach such an acceptance demands a history that deals equitably with those who were responsible for the course of history, which eventually led to our modern societies. It is the task of all those who long for a just and equal world to make sure that the role of women in human history is neither forgotten nor underestimated. The present book is part of this task and sheds more light on an important figure of the movement for women's rights since the dawn of the 20th century. One can only hope that it finds many readers and that the story of Mary Hunter Austin will give reasons for young women and men of the 21st century to continue the fight for true gender equality, in spite of those who still want to neglect the impact of women throughout human history and tend to solely emphasize the history of "old white men."

Bodø, March 2020
Frank Jacob

Introduction

Mary Hunter Austin (1868-1934) is usually considered as an important American writer of the early decades of the 20th century, whose well-known works deal with Native American culture and space, especially in Southern California and New Mexico. Nevertheless, the later US feminist movement reconsidered her to be an early feminist author whose works had an impact on the redefinition of gender roles during, and as an impact of, the First World War (WWI). She is described by modern scholars as an unusual voice in American literature who was gifted, eccentric, exasperating, tragic, elitist, and idiosyncratic.[1]

While it is correct to categorize Mary Hunter Austin as a proto-feminist writer, in the term's broadest sense, in her own time, her works were also impacted by the events of WWI, and this impact on Austin as a writer, activist, woman, and her 'feminist' views shall be taken into closer consideration in the present book. It will therefore offer a focus on some of Austin's works that have not been taken into close consideration yet, and will also show how Austin's relation to the proto-feminist movement during WWI would later transform her into a well-known and well-read figure among US feminists in later decades. How Austin's role as a war critic was related to her proto-feminist identity and her overall œuvre shall also be discussed.

The present research therefore selects some essential texts related to the time period in question, as Austin wrote them during or immediately after WWI. The texts were consequently chosen due to their chronological context to determine the war's influence on Austin's thoughts and opinions, not only expressed in her own literary works, but which the author often also voiced at rallies or in newspaper interviews. Timewise, the selection also overlaps with the war in Europe, as they were written before, during, and after the American interference. Therefore, I will look at how the war influenced the American writer's stand toward American intervention, the existent social order, and the role women played within the latter. Austin was a productive writer, thus there are many texts, plays, books, articles, and essays to choose from, but for the sake of sticking to the timeline, I do not intend to examine her entire life and works. Instead, I will provide a close reading for a time-limited case study of

---

[1] Esther Lanigan Stineman, *Mary Austin: Song of a Maverick* (New Haven: Yale University Press, 1989), 1.

Austin's writings and her criticism of WWI, including a special focus on gender-related issues she, as one of the early 20th-century agents of female emancipation, had criticized as well.

The essential texts that will build the text corpus of the present study are *The Ford* (1917),[2] *The Young Woman Citizen* (1918),[3] *No. 26 Jayne Street* (1920),[4] the political essay "Sex Emancipation Through War" (1918), as well as supplementary shorter newspaper articles published during the defined time period. Other important works that are of a notably 'feminist' character that will supplement this book and the discussion of Austin's later perception, but which do not fall into the WWI timeline, are Austin's autobiography from 1932, *Earth Horizon*,[5] and the work of fiction *A Woman of Genius* (1912),[6] in addition to contemporary newspaper essays and articles that discussed Austin's impact as a writer with regard to her role as an author and an activist.

Structure and Intention of the Work

This book will commence with a biographical chapter on Austin's life, motives, and experiences to show how her political identity formed over the years before WWI. After this biographical survey, a chapter will discuss the First World War in New York City, the war's impact on female anti-war movements, and Austin's life and works. After having mapped out these aspects, a close analytical reading of the four essential texts will be presented in chapter 3, followed by a final chapter discussing Austin and the feminist perception of her works in modern times. The chapters are arranged to go from biography to war experience to literature analysis, before finally presenting a discussion of Austin's commemoration and re-interpretation by feminists in the 1960s and 1970s. This will provide an insight into feminist "constructions of the past" as well as emphasize theoretical discussions about the creation of a collective memory that in a way also reflect upon the WWI experiences of American proto-feminists like Austin.[7]

The theoretical basis of this book is related to memory theory, reception theory, and the history of early 20th century US feminism in a broad sense.

---

[2] Mary Austin, *The Ford* (Boston/New York: Houghton Mifflin, 1917).
[3] Mary Austin, *The Young Woman Citizen* (New York: The Woman's Press, 1918).
[4] Mary Austin, *No. 26 Jayne Street* (Boston/New York: Houghton Mifflin, 1920).
[5] Mary Austin, *Earth Horizon: An Autobiography* (Boston/New York: Houghton Mifflin, 1932).
[6] Mary Austin, *A Woman of Genius* (New York: Doubleday, Page & Company, 1912).
[7] Anna Green and Kathleen Troup, *The Houses of History: A Critical Reader in Twentieth-Century History and Theory* (Manchester: Manchester University Press, 1999), 92-93.

Introduction xiii

The historical impact of WWI, although mapped out in its own chapter, will also be present throughout the book, as it is important to clarify its significance as a cultural watershed[8] in women's history in general and in Austin's individual case in particular. WWI and gender roles will consequently be looked at from a comparative perspective to analyze how the writer herself spoke of women's role in society in the developing years. She is perhaps one of the period's most significant female voices, as she documents her "journey of independence" from the Californian desert to her life as a single woman at the heart of political activism and commitments, which one can clearly read in the journalism about her.

Chapter 1 will provide insights into both who Mary Hunter Austin was and the main events of her life leading up to the timeframe of our research and focus. The chapter intends to show how the effects of her personal experiences impacted the literature that later also attracted or inspired members of the feminist movement. What makes Austin's biography special is that she was often allowed to tell her own story while others often played bystander roles. Among the important people in her life were her husband, mother, siblings, daughter, and many more, yet in many ways these people are often shadows of themselves, resulting in a characterization of the author as an almost self-centered yet also very dominant figure. It is her egocentricity and oddness that historian Abraham Hoffman criticizes in the concluding section "History vs. Literary Biography" of his article about Austin in the *Journal of the Southwest*.[9] Ultimately what the chapter critically puts forward is the idea not to trust all narratives; for example, despite Austin often claiming in her autobiography that she was unwanted by her family growing up, her being unwanted was not factual as a matter of scientific claim, but merely her own perspective and the voice of her adolescent loneliness. The importance of presenting a biographical chapter is to give readers an insight into who the late author was, as well as to be critical of how she saw herself.

The next chapter will present a short summary of the First World War in order to try to determine the impact of this war on Austin's works and growth, which are directly related to the war years and her respective experiences. The third chapter will then provide a close reading of the above-identified works and extract evident narratives that were presented within them to identify

---

[8] Some examples of the cultural impact of WWI can be found in Frank Jacob, Jeffrey Shaw, and Timothy Demy, eds., *War and the Humanities: The Cultural Impact of the First World War* (Paderborn: Schöningh/Brill, 2018).
[9] Abraham Hoffman, "Mary Austin, Stafford Austin, and the Owens Valley," *Journal of the Southwest* 53, no. 3/4 (2011): 319-320.

Austin's political positions in relation to her war experience, attempting to move the textual analysis away from modern re-readings and instead focus on the texts as truly to their intentions as possible. The narratives within the books shift with the years (1914-1920); for example, *The Ford* is socially and politically critical, like the two other books, but is also inspired by real events from the earlier 1900s. It is therefore important to take into consideration that, despite Austin taking inspiration from life around her until 1917 when it was published, the book's fundamental basis is from another time, yet it also highlights long-term conflicts within American society that had intensified and eventually erupted as a consequence of the war. This recollection of events, which are written about while being inspired by the current political climate, is something that occurs again and probably also more intensely with regard to the publication of *No. 26 Jayne Street*. This 1920 novel is a recollection of the war; thus, the author's narrative is carefully constructed around the experiences which she reminisces in its aftermath, thereby giving the narrative a wisdom that only a "post-experience" voice could.

The curious thing about Mary Hunter Austin's writing is that her stories, although rooted in fictional plots, often address larger ideas – e.g. gender roles or socialist philosophy – through individual experiences which are carefully connected to the single stories of the presented characters. The larger perspective of most of her writing is how she reflects on events and ideas in her life and around the world and then presents them in the form of people, perhaps because it is easier for a reader to connect to an individual than ongoing political debates without a heart to which they can relate the former and their own interest; this is particularly evident in *The Ford* and *No. 26 Jayne Street*, in which each character is carefully crafted to represent a political idea or agenda in themselves.

America's participation in the war definitely inspired Austin when she wrote *The Young Woman Citizen* in 1918, and its publication was made possible due to support from the Women's Press, whose editors actively went in to publish more books by women and for women in the period in question. The book is inspired by a time when women were eager to show their place in American society as men went to the battlefields in Europe. Austin reflects more directly on her politics and ideas in this book, which is similar to her journalism but unlike her other literary works, which deal less with political issues or debates. The most binding and interesting thing that this chapter will highlight is how utterly open to interpretation these books are, regardless of what era they are read in, thus making it evident as to why they are so open to modern (re-)readings.

The final chapter will then focus on the feminist perception and commemoration of Austin's work in later years and try to show why other works than those she wrote in relation to WWI were obviously more appealing

Introduction

to later feminists. The chapter will explore the idea of feminism and discuss the developments within the movement in the US during the 1960s and 1970s. Having established the historical context, the chapter will continue into the theoretical discussion regarding feminism, memory, and perception. The main goal of the chapter is to discuss literary reception, as well as memory and perception, in order to determine whether Mary Hunter Austin was correctly interpreted and perceived or not, and it will try to answer whether she was later constructed to be an early or proto-feminist writer. The chapter will consequently highlight the differences between the realities of the First World War and later feminist re-interpretations, with a special focus on Austin. The intent is to determine if the understanding of Austin (as a feminist) and her texts is more impacted by the redefinitions related to collective cultural memory or if it really is an appropriated interpretation of Austin's activities and her works, especially the ones in question for the present book. The theoretical discussion in this chapter must therefore also elaborate on feminism in its different historical forms or, better, stages of development.

Research Subject, Historiography, and Theoretical Reflections

Mary Hunter Austin is a significant research subject, because she was an important individual both in her own time and in times after her death. She concerned herself with matters of the geological and cultural landscape, women's rights, Native American rights, poetry, and matters of democracy and ethical issues alike. She was a prolific writer who produced short stories, novels, plays, essays, and articles, as well as being an activist on matters of nature, women, and war. Two years before her passing in 1934, Austin wrote and published her autobiography *Earth Horizon* (1932),[10] providing her own view on things she deemed more important than others, regardless of the image the public had of them. It is often claimed that Austin concerned herself with "feminist causes." The present study will refer to these more as "women's" causes than "feminist" ones, as it is important to note that "feminism," as the term will be used here, is not fully synonymous with its meaning and consideration in Austin's time. The research around Austin is often limited to her Native American prose and her best-known work, *The Land of Little Rain* (1903),[11] however the author was versatile in her literature and in her role in society, rather than being limited to just a few poems. In contrast to these more well-known works, the present study will explore

---

[10] Austin, *Earth Horizon*.
[11] Mary Austin, *The Land of Little Rain* (Boston/New York: Houghton Mifflin, 1903).

rather more ignored works by Austin and try to put them into their historical context and link them to their time of genesis and thereby the struggles women had waged for social justice and gender equality during WWI.[12] Austin often portrayed the struggle of imbalance between the two sexes, the construction of social gender roles, and the overpowering control of men. How her portrayals of imbalance and suchlike are of notable significance in modern interpretations will consequently be part of the analysis of her later perception. Nevertheless, the research question of the present book first and foremost focuses on the impact of the First World War on Austin's writings and the influence the war experience had on the gender roles represented in her war-related literature. Through analyzing her works from the period in question, the aim is to determine if later generations of feminist writers are truly justified in claiming the author's literature as being feminist in nature. The "women's movement," despite its long history even before our timeline, was able to reach tremendous political changes while Austin was able to observe and participate in the movement in her time. Therefore, it is with this in mind that this book should be read, as it does not attempt, nor claim, to tackle the entirety of Mary Hunter Austin's writings, but rather a small portion of them to answer the fundamental question about the creation of her political legacy as an activist writer in correlation with WWI.

In addition to Austin's main literary works in question, *The Ford* (1917), *The Young Woman Citizen* (1918), *No. 26 Jayne Street* (1920), and "Sex Emancipation Through War" (1918), the most important primary sources that this research is built on are contemporary newspaper articles. In regard to the quality of the literature specifically selected for its timely connection to the First World War, *The Ford* is related to its early years before the US intervened, *The Young Woman Citizen* was published during the global conflict, while *No. 26 Jayne Street* is significant as it provides an insight into the aftermath of the war. Thus, the selection is meant to provide a wide spectrum of both the author's standpoints as well as her perceptions of society in war-related contexts.

The Ford is included among the literature of importance because it was published during our period, however the work does not necessarily serve as a direct "war witness," as the plot is inspired by events unfolding in the earlier 1900s. *The Young Woman Citizen* and *No. 26 Jayne Street* are the works that we can directly connect to the war, as they are both, in a way, results of it. *The*

---

[12] For a broader discussion about the "women's question" and its link to left political movements in the late 19th and early 20th centuries, see Vincent Streichhahn and Frank Jacob, eds., *Geschlecht und Klassenkampf: Die "Frauenfrage" aus deutscher und internationaler Perspektive im 19. und 20. Jahrhundert* (Berlin: Metropol, 2020).

Introduction xvii

Young Woman Citizen showcases Austin's increased political engagement as a result of WWI and displays how the author became more outspoken about political matters not only in women's issues but about citizenship in general. *No. 26 Jayne Street* is important as it is a rewind of both the war and the research period. Ultimately, these books lay the ground for the present research and will be read to provide broader potential insights into Austin's intentions and voice.

As for the literature about the subject, rather than the literature that will be analyzed, the quality and quantity of previous research vary. When it comes to the literature available to date, the main positions and concepts when talking about Mary Hunter Austin have often been in regard to her nature-related or regionally focused writing, e.g. about California or New Mexico,[13] as well as to her position as a female teacher. For example, Abraham Hoffman's article about Austin, her husband Stafford Austin, and the Owens Valley, which also had a role in the events of a water crisis, focuses on the domestic portrayal of her life more than anything else and discusses the dynamic and unfolding of their story.[14] Hoffman quotes the author herself, saying, "I seem to be the sort of person about whom more myth than truth is in circulation."[15] If we take that quote, it serves as a purpose for Hoffman's paper. Its contribution to research on Austin is to question Mary Hunter Austin's feelings of superiority, focusing on what the author presented biographically and what was historically accurate, e.g. the plot of her book *The Ford*. Hoffman questions what the full truth is, because historically not all credit went where it was due, for example, to her ex-husband.

Hoffman's article encourages biographers and those who study any subject matter, in this case Austin and her war-related works, to be critical, rather than just to celebrate any greatness that is easily presented; for example, to be critical of how Austin gave very little credit to her husband Stafford in the fight for water rights in the later book adaptation of the events. Ultimately what Hoffman is attempting to discuss and criticize is the overwhelming optimism about Austin's achievements instead of questioning sources. The reason for this is that he believes many of the author's achievements in her efforts to secure water rights should have been credited to her husband and not her (such as "ignoring the fact that it was Stafford who contacted federal officials

---

[13] Oleh Heike Schaefer, *Mary Austin's Regionalism: Reflections on Gender, Genre, and Geography* (Charlottesville, VA: University of Virginia Press, 2004).
[14] Hoffman, "Mary Austin," 305-322.
[15] Ibid., 305.

about what was going on"[16]). Hoffman focuses on the events of her life that inspired *The Ford* and discusses the importance of knowing what is fact and what is fiction, despite Austin painting herself as the heroic character, which cannot be believed based on memory/perception without real biographical research.[17] Therefore, works such as *Exploring Lost Borders: Critical Essays On Mary Austin* by Melody Graulich and Elizabeth Klimasmith that offer a more critical approach will also be brought forth.[18] While Hoffman only focused on the events inspiring *The Ford*, the present analysis shall take a wider scope into consideration: the war era, the author's persona, her literature, and modern perceptions.

The focus points of the previous research are limited. While Hoffman centers on the real events inspiring *The Ford* and questions the reliabilities of biographies, others have also taken particular motivation points, such as in the article "Mary Austin and the Western Conservation Movement: 1900-1927" by historian Benay Blend, which goes into environmental issues and the claim of female space.[19] This research is important to create a deeper understanding of Austin as a person and author through a modern narrative, as her Native American writing and activism were not fueled by environmentalism per se but rather by the understanding of modernity. The presented research therefore intends to show that earlier studies focused on smaller, more specific things instead of providing an overall picture of Austin's development as a writer and activist.

Other interdisciplinary research of significance is provided by historian Karen S. Langlois, who has written about both personal and professional aspects of Austin's life over many decades and in different works. In 1986, Langlois could claim that "recently there has been a revival of interest in the American writer Mary Hunter Austin,"[20] making it clear that the research interest grew and declined in waves, which is noteworthy as the narratives of these different waves, namely during the 1960s and 1970s, are of special

---

[16] Ibid., 319. For more examples where the writer is credited for the discovery of water injustice without further criticism, see Gwen Sullivan, Review of *Mary Austin's Southwest: An Anthology of Her Literary Criticism*, by Chelsea Blackbird and Barney Nelson, *Rocky Mountain Review of Language and Literature* 60, no. 1 (2006): 126.

[17] Ibid.

[18] Melody Graulich and Elizabeth Klimasmith, eds., *Exploring Lost Borders: Critical Essays On Mary Austin* (Reno, NV: University of Nevada Press, 1999).

[19] Benay Blend, "Mary Austin and the Western Conservation Movement: 1900-1927," *Journal of the Southwest* 30, no. 1 (1988): 32.

[20] Karen S. Langlois, "Mary Hunter Austin and Lincoln Steffens," *Huntington Library Quarterly* 49, no. 4 (1986): 357.

interest to the present work. The recent revival, to name another of the waves, is related to the blooming interest in the US in the conservation and environmental protection of land and water during the period in which Austin wrote.[21] This is similar to the research presented by Esther Stineman, whose 1988 scholarly contribution is precisely about the subject of scholars (and society) continuously re-discovering Austin in different periods.[22]

Langlois' praise and research tributes to Austin continued, and in 1990, she published her article "A Fresh Voice from the West: Mary Austin, California, and American Literary Magazines, 1892-1910."[23] Her latest research on this subject, "Mary Austin and Andrew Forbes: Poetry, Photography, and the Eastern Sierra," was published in 2007.[24]

What Langlois brings to the field is specific and not always directly in tune with the "orthodox opinion" about Austin, however it improves the overall basis when attempting to profile her life, whether this is directly about the author or her harmony with other significant characters (such as Steffens or Forbes). Some of the research goes into feminism, using one of the modern definitions,[25] however the trend of the research is once again the female sex and landscape, in which Austin is repeatedly of great significance.[26] The same themes are present in Vera Norwood's work "Heroines of Nature: Four Women Respond to the American Landscape," published in 1984.[27]

---

[21] See also Nancy Cook, Review of *Exploring Lost Borders: Critical Essays on Mary Austin*, by Melody Graulich and Elizabeth Klimasmith, *Western Historical Quarterly* 32, no. 1 (2001): 96.
[22] Esther Lanigan Stineman, "Mary Austin Rediscovered," *Journal of the Southwest* 30, no. 4 (1988): 545-551. For more on the rediscovery of Mary Hunter Austin, see Catharine Savage Brosman, *Southwestern Women Writers and The Vision of Goodness* (Jefferson, NC: McFarland, 2016), 31-64.
[23] Karen S. Langlois, "A Fresh Voice from the West: Mary Austin, California, and American Literary Magazines, 1892-1910," *California History* 69, no. 1 (1990): 22-35.
[24] Karen S. Langlois, "Mary Austin and Andrew Forbes: Poetry, Photography, and the Eastern Sierra," *California History* 85, no. 1 (2007): 24-43.
[25] "Feminism is the refusal to define all women and therefore all human beings solely in terms of sex." Ginette Castro, *American Feminism: A Contemporary History* (New York: New York University Press, 1990), 2.
[26] Glenda Riley, "'Wimmin Is Everywhere': Conserving and Feminizing Western Landscapes, 1870 to 1940," *Western Historical Quarterly* 29, no. 1 (1998): 4-23.
[27] Vera L. Norwood, "Heroines of Nature: Four Women Respond to the American Landscape," *Environmental Review* 8, no. 1 (1984): 34-56.

In addition to her article "Mary Austin Rediscovered," Stineman is also the author of *Mary Austin: Song of a Maverick*,[28] a critical biographical work used as the basis for many discussions on Austin to come. Among those who further Stineman's work is Lois Rudnick, who in her article "Feminist on the Frontier"[29] writes that Stineman "examines Austin's life and work within a feminist framework that gives both positive and negative characteristics their due."[30] This enhances the point about the picture painted of Austin as predominantly feminist as a result of her life and work based on modern perceptions. This also leads to the necessity to include reception theory, which is a theoretical ground that will enhance our understanding of why the rediscovering of old texts and writers is a subjective matter for modern times. Reception theory is based on ideas such as those of Robert C. Holub, Hans Robert Jauss (1921-1997), and cultural theorist Stuart Hall (1932-2014), among others. These works all build on the idea of interpretation and how information, experience, history, and suchlike are sorted through perception.[31]

Austin's views on citizenship and her contribution to literature about social democratic themes in the 20th century are highlighted and discussed in Teena Gabrielson's "Women-Thought, Social Capital, and the Generative State: Mary Austin and the Integrative Civic Ideal in Progressive Thought," published in 2006.[32] This article is one of the most relevant pieces of research about the theme, as Gabrielson goes into the necessity for women going into politics and, thus, Austin's role in this development. A similar approach to the one of Rudnick reviewing Stineman can be found in Shelly Armitage's essay "Mary Austin's Regionalism: Reflections on Gender, Genre, and Geography by Heike Schaefer," in which Armitage argues that Schaefer makes it evident that "Austin cannot be understood nor valued unless reexamined in her own terms."[33]

---

[28] Stineman, *Mary Austin*.
[29] Lois Rudnick, "Feminist on the Frontier," Review of *Mary Austin: Songs of a Maverick*, by Esther Lanigan Stineman, *The Women's Review of Books* 7, no. 7 (1990): 22.
[30] Ibid.
[31] For further reading, see Stuart Hall, *Encoding and Decoding in the Television Discourse* (Birmingham: Centre for Contemporary Cultural Studies, 1973); Robert C. Holub, *Reception Theory* (New York: Routledge, 2003); Hans-Robert Jauss, *Toward an Aesthetic of Reception* (Minneapolis: University of Minnesota Press, 1982).
[32] Teena Gabrielson, "Woman-Thought, Social Capital, and the Generative State: Mary Austin and the Integrative Civic Ideal in Progressive Thought," *American Journal of Political Science* 50, no. 3 (2006): 650-663.
[33] Shelly Armitage, Review of *Mary Austin's Regionalism: Reflections on Gender, Genre, and Geography*, by Heike Schaefer, *Tulsa Studies in Women's Literature* 25, no. 1, (2006): 170.

Introduction

The 2004 book *Mary Austin's Regionalism: Reflections on Gender, Genre, and Geography*[34] by Heike Schaefer is one of the books that take a very similar approach to analyzing Austin to the present research, though less in terms of political impact, collective memory, and perception and more from a regional approach, as well as in seeking a balance between the author's many sides: "As a regionalist, Austin is thought to represent a female-dominated branch of realist writing, which celebrates communal ways of living and 'women's culture.' As a nature writer, by contrast, Austin is seen to work in a male-dominated tradition of environmental nonfiction, producing scientifically based and philosophically inspired texts."[35] It is described as "a critical study bridging fiction, nonfiction, and unpublished works,"[36] which is a similar method and approach to those used in this research. Through examinations similar to the ones conducted here, Schaefer argues that "Mary Austin's regionalism reestablishes the foundations of Austin's belief that at a truly democratic America only can realize itself through the knowledge and experiences of its formerly marginalized peoples."[37]

Other research done around Austin is often limited to journal articles exploring smaller aspects of her personality, none of which take a deeper analytical approach to her significance and influence on the time after her death and the impact of her contributions on a larger scale, most of them grounding themselves in the books published about the author.[38] The main point of interest seems to be the aspect of nature.[39] Shortly after her death, the author was described as an ego-centric (and ultimately ego-radiant) and epic person, however the research available does not do her justice.[40] On the topic of limitation, an example of the weakness of representation in regard to Austin's legacy is Augusta Fink's biography *I-Mary*, as it relies too much on Austin's own autobiography *Earth Horizon*, and thus one must begin to question the objectivity of the narratives provided. The weakness occurs because Fink trusts Austin's own autobiography as a source far too much in my opinion, however she still succeeds in drawing clean lines that tell the basic story of Mary Hunter

---

[34] Schaefer, *Mary Austin's Regionalism*.
[35] Ibid., 4.
[36] Armitage, Review of *Mary Austin's Regionalism*, 170.
[37] Ibid., 170-171.
[38] Augusta Fink, *I-Mary: A Biography of Mary Austin* (Tuscon, AZ: University of Arizona Press, 1983); Schaefer, *Mary Austin's Regionalism*; Stineman, *Mary Austin*.
[39] For further reading, see James Rupert, "Mary Austin's Landscape Line in Native American Literature," *Southwest Review* 68, no. 4 (1983): 376-390.
[40] Arthur E. DuBois, "Mary Hunter Austin 1968-1934," *Southwest Review* 20, no. 3 (1935): 242.

Austin's life. What the present research will contribute is to pinpoint the lack of objectivity when re-reading and exploring the impact of Mary Hunter Austin's literature related to the cultural impact of WWI and the memory of the early feminist movement, aspects not fully considered by the existent research. The present book therefore addresses research desiderata related to gender studies, the history of feminism, the history of the First World War, as well as the history of Mary Hunter Austin herself.

In addition to Austin's works and secondary literature, the research also relies on fundamental literature about the First World War, such as that of Sandra Adickes,[41] David M. Kennedy,[42] and Ross Wilson,[43] as well as works about socialism, such as "For White Men Only: The Socialist Party of America and Issues of Gender, Ethnicity and Race," written by Sally M. Miller in *The Journal of the Gilded Age and Progressive Era*.[44] Miller's work is fundamental as it both maps out the basics as well as brings forth the important discussion of limitations within socialism in terms of gender, which would apply to Austin. The most essential literature within the theories of collective memory is that of Maurice Halbwachs, Jan Assmann, and Pierre Nora,[45] which provide the leading theories and binding agents of the present research. Key literature also includes books on the First World War as empierced in the United States first and foremost, and then more specifically in New York, as it serves the purpose of informing about the political climate in the author's residential state at this time. It is not possible to explore all aspects of the war within the scope of one book, thus only focusing on reactions closest to Austin herself (in the United States to some degree, but mostly New York) is the most reasonable approach. The theories, as discussed by Nora in *Realms of Memory* (*Les Lieux*

---

[41] Sandra Adickes, *To Be Young Was Very Heaven: Women in New York Before The Great War* (London: Macmillan, 1997).
[42] David M. Kennedy, *Over Here: The First World War and American Society* (New York: Oxford University Press, 1980).
[43] Ross J. Wilson, *New York and the First World War* (Farnham: Ashgate, 2014).
[44] Sally M. Miller, "For White Men Only: The Socialist Party of America and Issues of Gender, Ethnicity and Race," *The Journal of the Gilded Age and Progressive Era* 2, no. 3 (2003): 283-302.
[45] For examples, see Jan Assmann, *Cultural Memory and Early Civilization* (New York: Cambridge University Press, 2012); Maurice Halbwachs, *On Collective Memory*, ed. Lewis A. Coser (Chicago: University of Chicago Press, 1992); Jacques Le Goff, "Mentalities: A History of Ambiguities," in *Constructing the Past*, eds. Jacques Le Goff and Pierre Nora (New York: Cambridge University Press, 2011), 166-180; Pierre Nora, "Preface to English Language Edition: From Lieux de memoire to Realms of Memory," in *Realms of Memory: Rethinking the French Past*, eds. Pierre Nora and Lawrence D. Kritzman, trans. Arthur Goldhammer (New York: Columbia University Press, 1996), xiii.

de Mémoire), make it possible to explore the impact of material or non-material matter becoming symbolic and of significance over time, thus allowing further discussions about perception.

Perhaps memory theory cannot stand the test of time alone in the big question we ask about Austin, and it is therefore the more complex combination of reception theory and memory theory that is required as a result of readers' responses when modern feminist identity was being built. Reception theory, as presented by scholar Robert C. Holub in his book *Reception Theory*, first published in 1982, builds on the idea of the reader's response, meaning the second-wave feminists' response to Austin and her peers. Although this theory might be weak in some respects, it is strong in the sense that Holub celebrates that this response is individual; thus, the reception of Austin is not collectively driven by someone larger and more mechanic, but by each individual woman, which obviously depends on different cultural factors, etc.[46]

In addition to Holub's work, essential theorists such as Martyn P. Thompson in his article "Reception Theory and the Interpretation of Historical Meaning"[47] discuss different theoretical interpretations of the historical meaning of literary reception and how readers create meaning, which ultimately explains the concept of giving meaning to texts, which Thompson refers to as "intentionalist."[48] In order to have a fully two-sided understanding of texts, it must be a mix of reception theory and the history of political thought to examine inconsistencies of literary reception when read by an intentionalist, and "by examining the one-sidedness of intentionalist theory in the light of a modified version of the reception perspective, it is shown that an understanding of historical meaning requires both insights."[49]

The original aim of reception theory (e.g. political thought) was to construct a theory of literary history that would be genuinely historical but which would not, in emphasizing the historicity of literary texts, fail to do justice to their artistic character as literary texts. This was in order to see if it is possible to write literary history and have it be both literary and history.[50] On the one hand, there

---

[46] Holub, *Reception Theory*, 82-84.
[47] Martyn P. Thompson, "Reception Theory and the Interpretation of Historical Meaning," *History and Theory* 32, no. 3 (1993): 248-272. For further reading, see John G. Gunnell, *Political Theory: Tradition and Interpretation* (Cambridge, MA: Winthrop, 1979), 96-129.
[48] Thompson, "Reception Theory," 248.
[49] Ibid.
[50] Rene Wellek and Austin Warren, *Theory of Literature*, 3rd ed. (Harmondsworth: Penguin Books, 1963), 252-253.

is the idea that "art has always reached its goal," which is very evident with regard to Austin's legacy, and that it is unwilling to accept that a history of writers, institutions, and techniques is appropriately literary and indeed historical literary history, thus concluding that literary history is impossible. On the other hand, Jauss argues that an appropriately literary and historical literary history can only be a history based on the aesthetics of reception.[51] It is this idea of the reception and creation of a history, particularly through the literary, which is thought-provoking. Austin fits Jauss' idea because she is illuminating as a person but also creating history through her literature, which resulted in creating tradition. Fiction was a crucial way for women to engage with politics at a time when their contribution was limited, especially in America, thus the literary and the political were unavoidably intertwined.[52] Scholars Gill Plain and Susan Sellers ask the question, "was there such a thing as feminist literary criticism in the Middle Ages?"[53] which we can apply to the more contemporary timeline to understand the creation of the modern feminist as a reinterpretation of formerly existent ideas or literary works. The critical feminist reading of Austin was part of a movement meant to lead to enlightened, progressive politics, and thereby a better world view through a social movement for the advancement of women.[54]

Modern feminist identity was built on the basis of Austin's persona and those of the likes of her, and scholars within the field of communication have taken into consideration how exploring identity can be done through media reception and power, and we can thereby make a link with Holub's idea of the "production of meaning."[55] Feminist literary criticism regards the feminist analytical project as a vital dimension of literary studies, and it aims to provide an accessible introduction to this vast and vibrant field.[56] The impact of feminism on literary criticism over the past thirty-five years has created a large transformation within the academic analysis. This is made evident in the findings in this book. By applying textual analysis and then combining feminist literary criticism with parts of reception and memory theory, one

---

[51] Thompson, "Reception Theory," 249-251.
[52] Gill Plain and Susan Sellers, *A History of Feminist Literary Criticism* (Cambridge: Cambridge University Press, 2012), 8.
[53] Ibid., 11.
[54] Ibid.
[55] Ibid., 1-2.
[56] Ibid.

gets a larger understanding of why Austin's books gained such a newfound response in modern readings: it was on the basis of new perceptions.[57]

The reason why Holub's work is unavoidably important is because American feminists of the Second Wave were not entirely drawing upon any direct memories, whether collective or individual, of Mary Austin's work or life, but rather how they comprehended these as they related to their own message. The majority of the works of Austin, and of many women of her generation, were forgotten in their own time but later got new life through the eyes of the new wave looking for feminist ancestors of sorts. Thus, they were deliberately unearthing writers whose works they did not know, appropriating them, and reshaping them for their own purposes; thus, it is fitting to consider reception theory here as it values the argument of how we subjectively pick up on what we want out of something. New introductions to Austin through re-prints and current debates sparked fresh interest, exemplarily through rediscovering "lost" treasures, which scholar Ann Funk describes as "presenting Austin to readers unfamiliar to her work,"[58] with reference to Stineman's work and revival of *Mary Austin: Song of a Maverick*. Funk claims that, in addition to the common presentation of Austin's work to those unfamiliar with it, Stineman also brings something new: texts not previously very accessible to the public. Among the titles is *Cactus Thorn*, a revival of her essay *One Hundred Miles on Horseback*.[59]

The reception of Austin's texts by feminists, i.e. for the purpose of creating a long-standing history of a feminist identity, is the reason why the texts chosen by feminists in later decades fall upon those in the war period, which in many ways limit this study, as Austin had many more texts that have directly fueled the modern feminist agenda. *The Ford, The Young Woman Citizen*, and *No. 26 Jayne Street* have been chosen here to narrow down the timeline, but also because they are the texts that run in parallel with the war period, meaning that modern re-readings were not only seeking directly female-related topics but also to analyze them in the context of extreme conditions such as war. The reception of the texts was simply created on the basis of their foundation: war led to putting pressure on active women such as Austin, which in turn resulted in radical texts. Austin ultimately imagined that her narrative and stories would have a hold on the future, despite this taking a little bit longer

---

[57] Holub, *Reception Theory*, 53-82.
[58] Ann Funk, Review of *A Mary Austin Reader*, by Esther Lanigan, *The Antioch Review* 54, no. 4 (1996): 494.
[59] Ibid. For further reading, see Mary Austin, *Cactus Thorn* (Reno, NV: University of Nevada Press, 1994); Mary Austin, *One Hundred Miles on Horseback* (California: Dawson's Book Shop, 1963).

than she might have envisioned, since interest in her works and character died down for a while before their rediscovery.[60] Schaefer writes about how Austin's belief in herself was eventually made possible because of feminist literary critics such as Graulich, Norwood, Stineman, Rudnick, etc. making new discoveries, which this time around included the late author, who had previously been excluded "when American literary criticism underwent a process of professionalization and concomitant masculinization in the thirties and forties."[61] An important theoretical point to look at here is that the building of identity, regarding the building of the 'self' both as an individual as well as collectively, is based on the relationship between individuals and the collective masses, with the takeaway being that each moves the debate about feminism and identity forward.[62]

Other examples of the rediscovery of and new interest in Mary Hunter Austin during the 1960s are evident in J. Wilkes Berry's article "Mary Hunter Austin (1868-1934),"[63] where the author discusses critical history and writes about the common notion wherein more attention is often given to the person of Austin than to her literature.[64] This "tendency to emphasize Mrs. Austin's personality at the expense of her writing"[65] highlights the point that the perception of feminist literature above all else also "renewed scholarly interest in Mrs. Austin's work," despite the fact that "published criticism remain[ed] meager" at that time (1969).[66]

Another instance where the new discovery was rather direct is Esther Lanigan Stineman's book *Mary Austin: Song of a Maverick*, where she writes in such a way that the words seem to continuously discover content about Austin that has not been seen or heard before, for example: "Austin in *The Arrow Maker* foregrounds her deep resentment over the enormous and stupid

---

[60] Schaefer, *Mary Austin's Regionalism*, 12.
[61] Ibid., 13.
[62] Margaret A. McLaren, "Two Feminist Views on the Self, Identity and Collective Action," *Hypatia* 14, no. 1 (1999): 120.
[63] J. Wilkes Berry, "Mary Hunter Austin (1868-1934)," *American Literary Realism, 1870-1910* 2, no. 2 (1969): 125.
[64] Ibid.
[65] Ibid.
[66] Ibid., 130. For more examples of works from the period, see Dorothy J. Altman, "Mary Hunter Austin and the Roles of Women" (PhD diss., State University of New York at Albany, 1979). For examples of works after Austin's death, see Dudley Taylor Wynn, "A Critical Study of the Writings of Mary Austin (1868-1934)" (PhD diss., Graduate School of Arts and Science of New York University, 1941), 1-22.

Introduction xxvii

waste of the gifts of women,"[67] which shows that books such as this (written in 1989) were written in a textually analytical way rather than in a directly biographical fashion, similar to *Earth Horizon* itself. The work of Stineman, as one of the key scholars in the rediscovering of Austin, is something we witness in many reviews as well, such as the above-mentioned one by Ann Funk, which states that *Song of a Maverick* both reminded people of what they had forgotten (e.g. Austin's early works) as well as brought works that had gone unnoticed back to the surface.[68] Since a further interpretation of Austin's life and work would not be possible without looking at the impact of the former, the following chapter will provide a biographical sketch of Austin for those who are not too familiar with her biography.

---

[67] Stineman, *Mary Austin*, 116.
[68] Funk, Review of *A Mary Austin Reader*, 493-494.

Chapter 1
Mary Hunter Austin (1868-1934): Life and Works

It is important to note that this chapter is both biographical as well as analytical. It does not provide a direct timeline, but rather a discussion of the life and motives of Mary Hunter Austin, which found their way into her literary works as well. As there are plenty of biographical works on Austin,[1] the present chapter rather intends to highlight the links between Austin's private life and the characters she would later present in her works, especially the ones taken into consideration in the next chapter. In her 1932 autobiography, *Earth Horizon*, Austin writes that she embarked on the mission of writing her own story with great pleasure and expectations, as she had believed it would be a joyous reminiscing of her journey and youth. The American scholar and writer Esther Stineman comments on this statement by emphasizing that "Austin had many reasons to write her story, not the least among them was to vindicate herself from the onus of deserting her husband and placing her child in an institution, personal agonies that colored her writing and career."[2] Austin vividly describes that, long before it was clear that she would become a fiction writer, not only for people but for the scenes, for nature, and for the mythical, and long before she could name these expressions, she wanted to write. The reason for this realization came as a result of not being able to express herself easily to others. The later author confirms that she felt misunderstood and that writing was a way for her to express herself in a wholesome manner and pay her respects to all the things she saw in a way others did not.[3]

---

[1] E.g., Austin, *Earth Horizon*; Fink, *I-Mary*; Susan Goodman and Carl Dawson, *Mary Austin and the American West* (Berkeley/Los Angeles; University of California Press, 2009); Lawrence Clark Powell, "A Dedication to the Memory of Mary Hunter Austin 1868-1934," *Arizona and the West* 10, no. 1 (1968): 1-4; Stineman, *Mary Austin*; Elizabeth Wright, "Mary Hunter Austin (1868-1934)," in *American Women Writers 1900-1945: A Bio-Bibliographical Critical Sourcebook*, ed. Laurie Champion (Westport, CT: Greenwood Publishing Group, 2000), 12-19.
[2] Stineman, "Mary Austin Rediscovered," 550.
[3] Austin, *Earth Horizon*, 1-3.

In order to move forward and to understand the mind of Mary Hunter Austin, and, thus, her writing, one must know her personal story.

Mary Hunter was born on 9 September 1868 in Carlinville, Illinois to parents George Hunter (1830-1878) and Susanna Graham Hunter (1840-unknown), and was a notable American landscape writer and later feminist icon. Growing up, the young author-to-be had many personal struggles, which included the hardships of never connecting with her mother and later the loss of her father, with whom she had a close relationship. These various traumatic aspects of her childhood had a tremendous impact on her spirit both positively (e.g. making her resilient) as well as negatively (e.g. making her disconnected from her family).

In her autobiography, Austin notes that her mother would often say, "I think the child is possessed!"[4] She did not understand or appreciate her daughter's vivid imagination or her lack of self-control in speaking whatever was on her mind, dismissing social cues of politeness – much to her mother's frustration and dismay. Naturally, the wedge between mother and daughter continued well into adulthood, and their relationship never developed in a positive manner.

The strain between mother and daughter continued after the author lost her father when she also lost her little sister, Jennie, whom the author describes as her best friend. This relationship was especially important to her as it was her most cherished one after the loss of her father, when Jennie was the one that took over George's role as her comforter and closest companion. In *Earth Horizon*, it becomes clear that Jennie's death severely impacted her.[5] Many years later, she described her reaction to the events as follows: "For once Mary had nothing to say; she laid herself dumbly against the sharp edge of sorrow, fearful that she would miss, as she thought she had missed her father's last moments, the least aching instant of loss."[6] The reason for feeling guilt and such pain about her sister's death was because she had developed a sore throat that same December, which had gone unnoticed by her mother and which later infected her sister.[7] Fifty years later, Austin described her sister as "the only one who ever unselfishly loved me."[8]

Upon losing her father and sister, she was in many ways an outsider in her own family. This resulted in some level of mental isolation, and from an early

---

[4] Ibid., 9.
[5] Ibid., 20-21.
[6] Austin, *Earth Horizon*, 86.
[7] Fink, *I-Mary*, 20-21.
[8] Ibid., 21.

age Austin developed an alter-ego, a braver and bolder version of herself, referred to as "I-Mary," which to her was more than just Mary-by-herself. She (I-Mary) had no need to be understood and did not mind being different: "To be I-Mary was more solid and satisfying than to be Mary-by-herself."[9] She clothed herself in this armor and felt brave whenever she needed to be stern and confident during the upcoming years of her life into adulthood.

Growing up, Austin's brother Jim Hunter, whom she went to school with, was the one who challenged her intellectually more than anyone, as they would argue about everything that one could argue about, and this helped to strengthen her through challenge. Among the author's many annoyances was that she felt that he was a priority for her mother because he was a boy. The result of the banter and constant competition for their mother's approval motivated Austin in her fight for women's causes. Years later, when the women's suffragette movement was at its peak and women all spoke of how they came to be active, Austin wrote in *Earth Horizon* that it was a four-minute egg that got her going and made her a woman who put her foot down. The story of the egg was one about her brother always determining how long the egg boiled for in the morning on behalf of everyone.

The experience of soft-boiled eggs unsettled her in the morning, and upon asking if her egg could be boiled for a minute or two longer, the request was not received positively. It became a constant annoyance and led to comments from Jim, who was the head of the house as he was the eldest son, such as "somehow you never seem to have any feeling for what a home should be,"[10] or her mother, such as, "Oh, Mary, why do you always have to have something different from the rest of the family."[11] This unfair division of authority based on gender seems to have motivated her through sheer frustration. However, it is important to note that she did not side with the suffragette movement, or general women's movements, for the entirety of her life, as she later evolved out of it.[12]

The writer was also different from other children, not just her family members. For instance, she could already read when she started school, which was something she had got from her father, who had exposed her to the works of William Shakespeare (1564-1616), John Keats (1795-1821), and Percy Bysshe Shelley (1792-1822), as well as popular American authors such as Herman Melville (1819-1891), Henry Wadsworth Longfellow (1807-1882), and Ralph

---

[9] Austin, *Earth Horizon*, 47.
[10] Ibid., 129.
[11] Ibid.
[12] Blend, "Mary Austin and the Western Conservation Movement," 14.

Waldo Emerson (1803-1882).[13] Her peers at school regarded her with a mixture of awe and suspicion because of her ability to read before she had started school, and she skipped grades straight into the third grade.[14] Regardless of these repercussions, pursuing an education was a passion supported by her late father, and with all the ups and downs in the Hunter household, she still succeeded in never giving up on her desire to finish school.

In 1888, after she had graduated from Blackburn College, her family packed everything up and moved to Southern California to seek land and a better life.[15] Nobody had consulted the young Mary Hunter about this move, which had been led by her brother, who had come to the decision after visiting some family in Pasadena in 1887.[16] The author convinced herself that she was indifferent to it, however as time passed it became clearer that she was perhaps less positive about it than she had initially thought, which became yet another strain between her and her family.[17]

However, Mary Hunter identified with the West and said of it that "everything seems so alive and insists on itself."[18] She could relate to this in many ways as she thrived on insisting on herself, trying to make ends meet as well as establishing her essence throughout her own life. Despite the hardship the Hunters experienced in the land, the writer was content because the unconventional society (e.g. the wilderness) felt more suited to her.[19] The term *normal* to specify averageness was not something that had yet been categorized, however the idea that there was a human norm, and that this norm was 'the average man,' was set; thus, a display of difference from women was categorized as a weakness of the female sex and of their intelligence, both mental and physical.[20] She defined stereotypes of women at the time by being outspoken on matters where women did not have a big role, such as the environmental issues present in her activism and literature, and is described as creating a "feminist alternative to the masculinist myths of the

---

[13] Fink, *I-Mary*, 13.
[14] Ibid., 16.
[15] Blend, "Mary Austin and the Western Conservation Movement," 12-34.
[16] Fink, *I-Mary*, 33-35.
[17] Ibid., 39-49.
[18] Blend, "Mary Austin and the Western Conservation Movement," 16-17.
[19] Ibid.
[20] Melody Graulich, "Mary, Mary, Quite Contrary," *The Women's Review of Books* 1, no. 4 (1984): 16-17.

far West as a place where men achieved heroism either by conquering the wilderness or by communing with it in solitary ecstasy."[21]

Mary Hunter Austin was peculiar in many ways from an early age, and this statement remains valid when it came to the opposite sex, because despite having an interest in boys, they seemed less keen on her because of her peculiar characteristics. After the Hunter family moved, it seems as though her mother was losing hope about her daughter ever finding a potential husband, and things did not look more optimistic when the late author turned down a marriage proposal in the midst of her mother's distress, who was then convinced that all hope was lost: "Well, I've brought you out here where there is nobody of your sort to marry..."[22] Perhaps the anguish in this situation was in many ways due to her wanting her daughter to lead a 'normal' and happy life, but it was also due to the financial struggles they were constantly facing. During this period, the young Mary Hunter's desire to write was growing because she was fascinated by the rich nature around her; thus, she spent her days merely enjoying herself.

In 1889 the recent college graduate applied for her first teaching job, which in many ways brought her back to reality, in contrast to how she had spent her days since the move (e.g. writing and enjoying nature all day).[23] The hardship of life as an adult in Bakersfield is also where she years later got her inspiration for *The Ford*, as the book's main events were driven from personal experience when two large land corporations were holding claim to the distribution of water rights in San Joaquin Valley.[24] She felt connected to the cause because of her experience with the drought on the land not too many years previously. There are resemblances between Austin's fiction, in this instance *The Ford*, and her political involvement, for example with regard to the water crisis, and the reason this is interesting is because it is another example of how she continued to intertwine her life and her fiction – something she did through most of, if not all, her works. Austin's views and interests in the West have been called "impractical to economists, legislators, and businessmen," who focused on the economic possibilities of the Southwest, yet she continued to persist and take space alongside such individuals.[25] Austin, despite the label of impracticality, was still passionate to the point where such impracticality did not matter and the cause made sense.

---

[21] Rudnick, "Feminist on the Frontier," 22.
[22] Fink, *I-Mary*, 50.
[23] Ibid., 50-53.
[24] Ibid., 52-53.
[25] Blend, "Mary Austin and the Western Conservation Movement," 21.

Throughout her life, Austin became tremendously dedicated to finding solutions and putting an end to the conflict between nature and culture. She wanted to find the fundamental value of nature and therefore wished to overcome hierarchical traditions in Western culture that imply the desert is a wasteland or that men control nature, and in the process, she became an advocate for Native Americans.[26] These values of hers started in the early stages of her youth. One can argue that because of the lack of emotional support from her family and later in life her husband as well, she looked to the flora and fauna of the desert for clues to survive under difficult conditions. Independent and self-defined, even borderline selfish and self-centered, her attitude often made her an outcast in the various Western towns where she lived during her lifetime. Consequently, Austin shared with other desert appreciators the strong sense of herself as a nonconformist who sought comfort in the spirituality provided by the land.[27]

In 1890 it became known that she had been excluded from any Hunter inheritance decisions, which she deemed absolutely unfair, as she saw it only right that she and her older brother would get an equal amount of help to start their lives – and equal say in how the family inheritance would be used (i.e. Austin's brother and mother made all the financial decisions without any consultation from her). In many ways, Austin realized that her 'only' option to build a life of her own was to get married.[28] However, this, i.e. matters of marriage, was also something that she did not jump into, but had been weighing up for years.[29] She gained newfound confidence when she met Stafford Wallace Austin (1862-1931), a neighbor who took an interest in her. He was seven years older than her, and Mary described him as "very absent minded but [an] extremely intellectual man."[30] This set the tone for the rest of their relationship; despite intellectual stimulants and practical properties to build a life, there was little romance. The courtship was anything but wild and was labeled as "modest love."[31]

Stafford provided and seemed to give more than enough, but although there was still no passion or fire, the wedding took place at the Hunters' estate in Bakersfield on 19 May 1891. It does not appear to have been a lavish or highly joyous day; the bride wore a plain brown dress that was

---

[26] Norwood, "Heroines of Nature," 41.
[27] Blend, "Mary Austin and the Western Conservation Movement," 16-17.
[28] Fink, *I-Mary*, 54.
[29] Austin, *Earth Horizon*, 220.
[30] Ibid., 54-55.
[31] Ibid., 56.

meant for function, not fashion.[32] One can argue that the day set the dull tone for the rest of their marriage.

Despite the notion that "Mary's husband was more than ordinarily lacking in the sense of the passing of time,"[33] the author's selfishness from her girlhood also continued into the marriage, and it became clear that she did not enjoy making a home. She hated housework and let the family live in a mess so she could focus on her writing. To say that the couple 'functioned' would be a big overstatement as they lacked communication, and it became clear that their attempt to live a farm life was not going to work out. Stafford was not a talented farmer, and his wife did not care for the household, thus tension was created. Despite the lack of much joy, success, or structure in their marriage, the couple had a child in the spring of 1892.[34]

Financial difficulties continually pestered the new Austin union, which led to many moves in order to provide more permanent economic solutions for the family. When Stafford's brother suggested they move to San Francisco in order to pursue a job opportunity, it was without hesitation that the family parted ways. The plan was for Mary to follow when everything was set, but in the meantime, not having to take another person in the house into consideration, she spent her time constructing and publishing two short stories. The stories were inspired by and based on her observations from her time in Tejon in Kern County.[35] The first short story was *The Mother of Felipe* (1892), which was the more gloomy of the stories, about a Mexican mother's refusal to leave her dead child in a desert grave.[36] The second story was *The Conversion of Ah Lew Sing* (1897), which served as a more lighthearted one and was an amusing story about a Chinese truck gardener.[37]

The accomplishment of selling these stories gave her a great sense of triumph and confidence, and she described it as an "opening movement of an activity that was to mean more to me than anything that was ever to happen to me; quietly as I suppose all growing things begin."[38] The confidence in her achievements gave her the ease to follow Stafford anywhere, knowing that she

---

[32] Ibid., 59.
[33] Hoffman, "Mary Austin," 307.
[34] Fink, *I-Mary*, 59-63.
[35] Ibid., 61-62.
[36] Mary Austin, "The Mother of Felipe," *The Overland Monthly* 20 (1892): 534-538.
[37] Mary Austin, "The Conversion of Ah Lew Sing," *The Overland Monthly* 30 (1897): 307-312. See also Hsuan L. Hsu, *Geography and the Production of Space in Nineteenth-Century American Literature* (New York: Cambridge University Press, 2010), 114.
[38] Fink, *I-Mary*, 62.

could always write.[39] Thus, began the journey of the twenty-four-year-old, pregnant, and recently published Mary Hunter Austin, in pursuit of her husband, to the Owens Valley, specifically to Lone Pine, east of the Sierra Nevada.[40]

If there was anything that the writer truly enjoyed in her new surroundings, it was the nature of the Eastern Sierra in the spring of 1892: "The origin of mountain streams is like the origins of tears, patent to the understanding but mysterious to the sense."[41] Despite the fresh start, history began to repeat itself for the family as the job that they had initially moved for went downhill, and they were left without income and unable to pay for their residency at the Lone Pine Hotel. They therefore moved to a boarding house on the outskirts of town.[42] The boarding house was not a good home, and the situation was less than ideal; consequently, the pregnant Hunter Austin decided to travel back to Bakersfield to deliver her baby in familiar surroundings with her mother and the rest of the Hunters by her side.

On 30 October 1892, Mary gave a taxing birth to her baby daughter Ruth, which led to a longer stay in Bakersfield.[43] In addition to her post-partum exhaustion, the new mother got the news that her husband had got them into extreme financial debt, some even from before their marriage, and that everything they owned was on credit. The Hunters were not fond of debt, deeming it disgraceful, and encouraged their daughter to get a divorce, but she refused. Although their marriage was dull in every way and their finances were a mess, she chose to stay. This decision was entirely based on the sole purpose of knowing that Stafford supported her goals of becoming a writer and knew that it would not be accepted with the same understanding in the Hunter household.[44] The theme of seeking freedom as an independent woman in exchange for personal hardship became a continuous one in her writing as her voice matured in her pursuits in literature.

Notwithstanding society's stereotypes, the hardworking writer took it upon herself to sort out the family's financial state, selling what could be sold, and regained some control of the situation, which can be described with a reversion of the quote by John Stuart Mill (1806-1873): "A man who is married to a woman his inferior in intelligence, finds her a perpetual dead weight, or,

---

[39] Ibid., 64.
[40] Ibid.
[41] Langlois, "Mary Austin and Andrew Forbes," 24.
[42] Ibid., 29.
[43] Fink, *I-Mary*, 70-71.
[44] Ibid.

worse than a dead weight, a drag, upon every aspiration of his to be better than public opinion."⁴⁵ In Mary Hunter Austin's case, it was in fact she who was dragging the dead weight of her husband (and his failures), thus disproving the stereotype.

Life appeared to finally get under control when Stafford Wallace Austin accepted a position as a superintendent of schools in the area. Their financial situation was still unstable due to the amount of debt, however, resulting in mother and daughter moving to Bishop, sixty miles north, to teach English, literature, and art at the Inyo Academy in order to provide two stable incomes.⁴⁶

Years later, when it was confirmed that Ruth was sadly permanently mentally disabled, the Hunter household provided no support to the Austins, and the only acknowledgment the daughter got from her mother was the following remark: "I don't know what you've done, daughter, to have such a judgment upon you."⁴⁷ This letter was the last contact between the two. She had in many ways wished for more understanding and support from her mother and less judgment on Ruth's behalf; she reminisced about the experience when stating that "I don't know what I expected: that she would penetrate to my suffering; that she would come to me and that we could wee and console one another…"⁴⁸

During her period in the Owens Valley (1892-1899), Austin found companionship in Miss Williams, with whom she became good friends, maybe because of their similarities, including them both being teachers as well as wanting to be writers. Miss Williams taught at an Indian school located in a reservation, and it was through her that Mary Austin got the opportunity to connect with the Native American population close by and got the benefit of visiting them on their land, much to her delight. During this time, Austin was made aware of the abuse and mistreatment that was happening to the Native Americans in the area (Paiute Indians).⁴⁹ For example, she got an insight into a practice called *mahala*-chasings, where Native American girls working in town as housekeepers were attacked on their way home from work. These attacks included beatings, as well as cases of rape and other

---

[45] John Stuart Mill, *The Subjection of Women* (Indianapolis: Hackett Publishing Company, 1988).
[46] Langlois, "Mary Austin and Andrew Forbes," 30.
[47] Austin, *Earth Horizon*, 357.
[48] Ibid.
[49] Fink, *I-Mary*, 84-87. For further reading on the tribes mentioned by Austin (among which are the Shoshone, Mojave, Washoe, Ute, Pomo, Pima, Yuma, Cohuelia, Apache, Yaqui, Papago, Navajo, and Pueblo), see Austin, *Earth Horizon*, 360.

unjust actions.[50] She used the opportunity to get in contact with the indigenous culture and to learn about it, as it 'spoke' to her. She also included these experiences in her writing and, later on, in her activism.

Melody Graulich writes that "Austin never attempted to separate her art from her politics, and she confronted such issues as the rape of Indian and Chicana women and spousal abuse at a time when such behavior was the 'norm.'"[51] Going against what was considered normal when 'normal' was not even an established concept is what determined Austin's life as an activist. This is clearly the case as it influenced the writer in her journey of self-discovery within the areas of politics and sociocultural understanding. Her political views on society were impacted by the injustice she saw in the male-dominated culture she was surrounded by. "Austin was always a political activist, so much so that her career as a writer may have suffered because of her commitment to a variety of social causes which seem now presciently in advance of her time."[52]

Austin's life in the Owens Valley was not the most joyous, and she was struggling between her teaching jobs and attending to Ruth's needs; thus, oftentimes, Ruth was left alone to fend for herself, which naturally did not go too well.[53] The writer realized her daughter's distress, and the two moved to Los Angeles in 1899.[54]

During this period, in which she was trying to take care of both herself and her daughter, she took the new environment as an opportunity to develop her writing skills with a greater sense of purpose, which led her to the mentorship of Charles Lummis (1859-1928). Lummis was a journalist and editor of the magazine *Land of Sunshine*, and he became an important part of the late writer and her daughter's lives.[55] At this point in time, Austin believed she was an established writer, however she needed encouragement and guidance, which Charles provided personally, in addition to giving her the advantage of becoming part of the Los Angeles circle of friends and writers involved in the world around Lummis and *Land of Sunshine*.[56]

---

[50] Fink, *I-Mary*, 84.
[51] Graulich, "Mary, Mary, Quite Contrary," 16-17.
[52] Blanche H. Gelfant, "'Lives' of Women Writers: Cather, Austin, Porter / and Willa, Mary, Katherine Anne," *NOVEL: A Forum on Fiction* 18, no. 1 (1984): 69.
[53] Fink, *I-Mary*, 80-81.
[54] Ibid., 95.
[55] Ibid., 96-100.
[56] Edwin R. Bingham, "American Wests through Autobiography and Memoir," *Pacific Historical Review* 56, no. 1 (1987): 10-11.

In 1902, the US Congress passed the National Reclamation Act to provide water to dry, inhospitable land in the West, and it was meant to lead to a substantial land reclamation project in the Owens Valley. The US General Land Office in Independence (who were behind the unfair acts of water claims) was also where Stafford was employed, and he was politically active in the county as well as in charge of handling the work around the project and all of its official records.[57] This incident is worth noting as it became the inspiration for some of Austin's writing in *The Ford* (1917),[58] as well as having a major impact on the breaking point in their marriage. Simultaneously, it became inevitable that Ruth could not be cured and was unhappy in the care of her mother, who did not wholeheartedly connect with her, and committing her to a high-ranked institution in Santa Clara became the solution.[59] Austin, despite the lack of connection, loved Ruth deeply and wanted her to live in a place where she could be happy and free, free of judgment from both other children as well as adults.[60] As practical as ever, she set out to provide money for this comfort she was seeking for her child and did so by selling her writing.[61] She selected several essays to sell by the page in order to provide money, including essays that later became part of her most famous book, *The Land of Little Rain* (1903).[62] This savvy-minded, strong mother made ends meet for her child, and in January 1904, Ruth was placed at the institution for a trial period to evaluate the quality this new life could provide for her flourishment and well-being.[63]

The events of the water crisis and the reclamation project directly led to the downfall of the Austin family, and by 1906 they had sold their shared house and separated for good. Although it would be a while before an actual divorce was finalized in 1914, they never rekindled their relationship in any way after the separation.[64] In the aftermath, Mary Austin moved to Carmel, California, and Wallace Austin eventually settled down in Trona in the Mojave Desert.[65]

Meanwhile, Mary Hunter Austin's writing was moving beyond its early focus on Native American tales, mining, and sheepherding traditions. This shift

---

[57] Langlois, "Mary Austin and Andrew Forbes," 24-43.
[58] Hoffman, "Mary Austin," 305.
[59] Langlois, "Mary Austin and Andrew Forbes," 42.
[60] Fink, *I-Mary*, 120.
[61] Ibid., 109.
[62] Ibid.
[63] Ibid., 120.
[64] Langlois, "Mary Austin and Andrew Forbes," 42.
[65] Ibid.

came when her marriage began to break apart in around 1905. Her literary skills matured into a new stage, focusing more on the hardship of women's lives in the West, a prime example being one of the stories in *Lost Borders* (1909), "The Bitterness of Women," which explores domestic relations gone wrong.[66] It paints a picture and explores how in "the treacherous desert country men are lost, children die, [and] women who wish to become wives and mothers live wasted lives."[67] This is the point from which the writer further evolves and deliberates more broadly on the theme of women not making a life for themselves without a man, into which she is not only projecting her own life but also putting other women's experiences into words. Among the subjects were the Native American women she encountered in the desert as well as her mentors, such as the novelist Charlotte Perkins Gilman (1860-1935), who was one of the influential people she met through her relations with Charles and his wife. Gilman served as a prime example of *what* Mary wanted to be: someone who had suffered an unhappy marriage, who had been accused of being an unsuitable mother, and who had had to give her children over into someone else's care, yet who was still fighting for the social and economic liberation of her gender.[68]

Politics, Philosophy, and People of Impact

There are many more details to the story of Mary Hunter Austin, like why she chose to settle down in Carmel, California of all places, and why she lived as she did. Her personal infatuation with the poet George Sterling (1869-1926) was one factor.[69] However, the move was not primarily about love or infatuation, but rather about where literature and politics took Mary Austin during the years leading to the First World War.

Having settled in California, without anyone holding her down, she became something of a wanderer, going to places such as England, Italy, France, and so on. Austin believed that it was only less sophisticated people who were immune to the evils of materialism and sexism, and she hoped their qualities would influence white society.[70] This was sadly a point she did not seem to reach, as her wandering was a kind of reaction to feeling that California had lost itself and the nature that had drawn her toward life there in the first place; the buildings and new scenery of modern society had strayed away from the

---

[66] Langlois, "A Fresh Voice," 32-33.
[67] Ibid., 33.
[68] Fink, *I-Mary*, 84-100.
[69] Ibid., 114-119.
[70] Blend, "Mary Austin and the Western Conservation Movement," 23.

naturalistic ideals she was more drawn to. Blend writes that she escaped this new reality by fleeing to Europe in search of a new identity and an environment she could connect with again. Among her adventures was learning about self-healing at a convent in Italy. The writer's list of connections within the literary world continued to expand in England, where she met George Bernard Shaw (1856-1950), W. B. Yeats (1865-1939), and H. G. Wells (1866-1946), just to mention a few of the important English and Irish writers in Austin's personal orbit.[71] Her 'feminist' intellectuality and properties developed greatly due to her attending a British socialist meeting of the Fabian Society in London.[72] This society was appealing not only because of the influential literary individuals that were involved but also because of their support for Austin's fundamental drive, and politics where women were concerned, as the Fabian Society was in support of the suffragette movement in Great Britain.[73] During these years, it was noted that strong ideas about gender equality and women's rights became further cultivated by her, and Austin's political views became more socialist.

The author was a firm believer that men's experience could not speak for women, as she thought that women's vision for 'selfhood' was considerably different from men's.[74] To quote Mill, in order to set this point clearly, "there is no subject on which there is a greater habitual difference of judgement between a man judging for himself, and the same man judging for other people."[75] Despite different experiences, by 1916, Austin believed that club women had failed to change and redefine American society because she did not see women as equal participators in a collective experience. Her belief was that women's fight was backfiring and that their organizations were slowing down in efficiency, deeming the overall female effort as powerless in their fight for social change.[76] The arguments go further with the conviction that the values women opposed in these groups were the very same that they also submitted to by being so heavily organized, thus leading to a loss of reliability and their actions only being perceived as a lighthearted pastime.[77]

---

[71] Gelfant, "'Lives' of Women Writers," 66.
[72] Blend, "Mary Austin and the Western Conservation Movement," 13.
[73] Derril Keith Curry Lance, "The Suffragette Movement in Great Britain: A Study of the Factors Influencing the Strategy Choices of the Women's Social and Political Union, 1903-1918" (MA Thesis, University of North Texas, 1977), 61.
[74] Graulich, "Mary, Mary, Quite Contrary," 17.
[75] Mill, *The Subjection of Women*, 104.
[76] Blend, "Mary Austin and the Western Conservation Movement," 14.
[77] Ibid.

When her time in England and Europe came to an end, Austin returned to the United States, namely New York City, where she befriended important intellectuals and writers, who inspired her further. Teena Gabrielson has argued that Austin's residency in New York was a deliberate act in the hope of better representing the West in literary circles.[78] When reading various sources and perspectives, the natural conclusion in this particular case is that her time in Europe, surrounded by important literary names, would provide her with reliability and attention back in the United States. What started out as an idea to represent the American West ended up developing her politically toward women's rights and questions of war and society in general. Austin describes herself as knowing English suffrage far better than American suffrage and described English women as having reached a point of revolt against maternity rather than impulse (in relation to birth control).[79]

In 1918, Henry Mills Alden (1836-1919), the editor of *Harper's Magazine*, took notice of Austin's increasing devotion to literary realism and detected that this modern literature was spectacular as it "focused on individual 'psychical motive' rather than the 'externality of life.' Its oath was 'truth in the interpretation of life.'"[80] This goes to show how the increase in notoriety was a steady process over time as she evolved as a writer. Her years in New York, and this evolved voice of realism, were also what stimulated *The Ford* (1917), *The Young Woman Citizen* (1918), and *No. 26 Jayne Street* (1920).

During her time in New York, she was, for a period, occupied with the European war and its potential developments; in one such effort, the author was involved in the conservation of food in a community kitchen. It was a time to express loyalty and contribute as much as possible, with the belief that Americans could stay out of the conflict.[81] When the United States entered the war in April 1917, Austin continued to volunteer for the food conservation efforts, going into this with the same understanding as the rest of the nation: that this was a war that would bring lasting peace.[82] This war was often referred to as the war to end all wars, and will be further discussed in the chapters to come.

The author's philosophy changed massively during the years of global conflict, not only in her literature but also in her general reality. Her literary works took a gradual leap from familial fiction, such as *Love and The Soul Maker* (1914),

---

[78] Gabrielson, "Woman-Thought," 651.
[79] Austin, *Earth Horizon*, 325.
[80] Langlois, "A Fresh Voice," 12.
[81] Wilson, *New York and the First World War*, 94-100.
[82] Fink, *I-Mary*, 172-186.

toward more politically themed books, such as *The Young Woman Citizen* and *No. 26 Jayne Street*, in both of which she encourages women not to be afraid to take up space and demand their rights in order to contribute toward a common American peace and prosperity. It should be noted that the latter is a fictional account of the war published in its aftermath, while the former is a political essay written during the height of the situation.

Individuals in New York were at the epicenter of American anti-war and otherwise pacifist efforts, which reflected on all things; arts, politics and life.[83] In the city, Austin was surrounded and inspired by like-minded individuals, and published works such as "Sex Emancipation Through War"[84] parallel with *The Young Woman Citizen*. These writings can also be regarded, in many ways, as further developing the ideas of Emma Goldman's 1911 publication *The Tragedy of Woman's Emancipation*.[85] Both of the works by Austin showcase her connection to other women similar to herself and give an indication of the type of intellectual woman she made connections with, whom she even described as "perfectly sound," despite her being a peasant.[86] Austin's description of Goldman as a peasant is perhaps in many regards why she is described as "elitist" by Stineman in modern readings.[87]

A notable figure the author describes herself keeping up with, who had a great impact on her ideas, was Charlotte Perkins Gilman. Austin named Gilman's work on women and the economy as notable and important.[88] It was in fact Gilman who introduced Austin to Goldman,[89] and the two are among only a few names the author drops in *Earth Horizon* as impactful on her ideas and relating to her network of women.[90] The networks between these women are what allowed for their strength in numbers, and it was through introductions and social events that they came to unite in ideas, e.g. luncheons hosted by various

---

[83] Adickes, *To Be Young Was Very Heaven*, 11-12. For further reading on anti-war activism, see Susan R. Grayzel, "Men and Women at Home," in *The Cambridge History of the First World War*, vol. 3: *Civil Society*, ed. Jay Winter (Cambridge: Cambridge University Press, 2014), 112-113, 118-119.
[84] Mary Austin, *Beyond Borders: The Selected Essays of Mary Austin*, ed. Reuben J. Ellis (Carbondale, IL: Southern Illinois University Press, 1997).
[85] Emma Goldman, *Anarchism and Other Essays*, 2nd ed. (New York: Mother Earth Publishing Association, 1911), 219-231.
[86] Austin, *Earth Horizon*, 326.
[87] Stineman, *Mary Austin*, 1.
[88] Austin, *Earth Horizon*, 325.
[89] Ibid., 326.
[90] For further reading on notable women Austin names as friends or having been introduced to, see ibid., 325-329.

entertainers, such as "the women's Cosmopolitan Club in honor of Dr. Anna Howard Shaw."[91] These were among the places that Austin would gather to discuss ideas and such with other active women, for example Anne Howard Shaw (1847-1919), an acquaintance of Austin and an important suffragist leader herself at the time. These types of luncheons were not uncommon, and in a letter from Austin, addressed to Elisabeth Garver Jordan a year later, she writes, "I certainly won't miss one of your luncheons if I can help it,"[92] indicating that these types of networking social events were a big part of Austin and Jordan's relationship, as well as of the circle of which they were a part. In many of the letters Austin wrote to Jordan, it is obvious that they discuss her writing as part of their socializing as both writers and editors, friends, and social activists.[93] The impact of the First World War on Austin led to her engagement in feminist causes and demonstrations all over the world and the United States, and therefore it is no surprise that the novelist's political and intellectual drive became more focused on asking women the questions of *what* they were contributing to society and *how* they could supply the nation.[94] Despite the United States not entering the global conflict until years after the breakout of the war, its influence was still ever-present where matters of identity and citizenship were concerned.[95] And this is where Austin's drive was the most present, as she was engaged in matters of citizenship. Despite being something of a pacifist herself, what made Austin different was her willingness to compromise for potential eternal peace and to aid American democracy.

Mary Hunter Austin was a woman who was constantly fighting a battle, whether it was a personal one behind closed doors or a political, social, or literary one in public. The writer did not seem to know how to rest, and despite Austin's writings being primarily works of fiction, the main focus being landscapes and Native American culture and rights, she was a writer who matured and developed. The years prior to the war were a time in which she unapologetically developed her sense of self and her social and political ideals in order to give back. One can argue it was not the war itself that induced her to write books in favor of women during the period under study but the years preceding it, during which she built her fundamental beliefs that were enhanced under the circumstances.

---

[91] "Luncheon in Dr. Shaw's Honor," *The Sun*, April 14, 1914, 9.
[92] Mary Hunter Austin to Elizabeth Garver Jordan, New York, March 18, 1915, New York Public Library, Rare Books and Manuscripts, Elizabeth Garver Jordan Papers, Box 1, Folder 6, 1.
[93] Ibid.
[94] Kennedy, *Over Here*, 30-35.
[95] Wilson, *New York and the First World War*, 15.

One can unquestionably claim that Mary Austin refused to conform to the standards that society had set for her; she was living in a world of her own, and her attitude was one of resistance toward following female stereotypes from youth into adulthood. The post-World War narrative had indeed given her new life with the growth of the concept of feminism and the new gender roles at the time. However, claiming Austin's intentions to be predominantly feminist would be too limited as she was not bound by such terms, even if her fight contained the evolution and pursuit of freedom for women. Despite the narratives in her various works having assertive feminist undertones, the interpretation is always in the hands of the reader. Perhaps the moral of her story is that readers did not grasp her intentions until much later than she had envisioned. These ideas are ones that we see in her fiction both long before the war, such as *A Woman of Genius*, and even more after it, such as in *Earth Horizon* (1932).

First published in 1912, *A Woman of Genius* is more or less a fictional autobiographical novel that follows the life of protagonist Olivia Lattimore, many also claiming the book as a dress rehearsal of Austin's personal life and upcoming Autobiography.[96] It begins, much like Austin's origin, in a small town named Taylorville in Ohianna (a fictional town placed in the Midwest), where Olivia spends her childhood and youth until she marries. This life, as one can imagine, is shackled and does not provide Olivia with the freedom she wishes for in her pursuit of existence, if anything. Olivia manages to escape this life in invisible shackles, which ultimately frees her to spread her wings as she becomes an actress in London and New York, similarly to Austin herself, and gains notoriety. Many consider the book as feminist because it draws on the life of a character who chooses herself, her freedom, and her career over a dull life. This novel is exactly what Austin wished she could balance in life and career as *A Woman of Genius*.[97] The main character's (Olivia's) rejection of a marriage proposal is one that can be labeled as advancing the idea of 'the new woman'[98] – which is also evident in Austin's own life in the many cases where she did not settle for the first man to ask for her hand in marriage. The vision of strong independent women continued to emerge in her stories, e.g. in the short story "The Walking Woman."[99]

---

[96] Stineman, *Mary Austin*, 136.
[97] "Great value for 29c: 4 for $1.00," *The Sunday Star*, July 12, 1914, part 1.
[98] Stineman, *Mary Austin*, 143.
[99] Janis P. Stout, "Mary Austin's Feminism: A Reassessment," *Studies in the Novel* 30, no. 1 (1998): 100.

Earth Horizon was published twenty years later and contains many of the same themes of how the author came to grow up: the death of her father and sister, the problems and lack of friendship with her mother, the strained relationship with her brother Jim, and the failure of her marriage, for which she largely seems to blame her husband for his lack of character and ability to provide.[100] However, it is always evident that Austin is grateful for having escaped life in Carlinville, which was only possible because of marriage and eventually her writing.

On the subject of her marriage, Austin writes that married life was nothing like what she had expected, as it was rather disappointing. The topic of her disappointment in marriage became rather clear in the years to come with headlines in newspapers that printed the author's opinions on marriage, such as "Mrs. Mary Austin Advocates Schools for Lovers to Lessen the Divorce Evil."[101] Austin is quoted as saying that real love is finding the right kind of marriage in which you marry a person you love, "to marry the person who one loves and by whom one is loved, to keep on loving and being loved so long as both do live – that is the only perfect and possible ideal for men and women."[102] The author of the article, Marguerite Mooers Marshall, is evidently an independent writer who discussed what had previously been written in other articles about young people marrying without critical thinking and ending up in divorce. Ironically, this came two years before Austin's own divorce was finalized. This progressive thinking is radical for its time and continued to paint Austin as a wise yet modern voice.[103] Marshall continues the article by writing that Austin's solutions are so beyond her time that she is perhaps either one of the most radical reactionaries or one of the most reactionary radicals.[104] Ultimately, it is on the basis of public appearances such as this that one can consider that Austin's personal experience clearly colored her works, even those relating to the war, which shall soon be looked at more closely. Earth Horizon is written in the third person, in her "I-Mary," and for this reason, it almost feels like it is a work of fiction, but the Austin who wrote Earth Horizon has clear definitions of who she was in different periods of her life.

---

[100] Austin, Earth Horizon, 227.
[101] Florence E. Yoder, "Mrs. Mary Austin Advocates Schools for Lovers to Lessen the Divorce Evil," The Washington Times, July 31, 1914, 11.
[102] Marguerite Mooers Marshall, "Mate Love, Only Basis for Happy Marriage, Can Be Recognized by Three High Signs," The Evening World, February 18, 1914, 3.
[103] Ibid.
[104] Ibid.

It is perhaps problematic to take any of these books at face value because Austin paints Olivia in the image she saw for herself, while *Earth Horizon* is written in the past tense, which paints her as perhaps more self-aware than she ever was in the real moments of her life. Consequently, the reason why books such as *Earth Horizon* will not be handled here is not only because they do not fit the timeline but also because they are more reflections in an omniscient voice, in which Austin defines her own most valuable moments in hindsight, e.g. clearly defining her own 'feminism' in the book (and its index)[105] when she was not even aware of this feminism at the time in question.[106] Austin is quite direct about the fact that she only writes about everything that she believes matters, and thus even the collection of information is subjective, not just the narrative.[107] Austin's ideas of equal marriage and strong-willed women have been red lines throughout all of her fiction, from *The Ford*, *26 Jayne Street*, and *A Woman of Genius* to her political essays that contain women freeing themselves of their shackles and claiming citizenship and the freedom of waged labor; however, these definitions only become clear later on and are evidentially less so at their respective times.

Austin After the War

Austin's proto-feminism and writing continued to flourish after the war; in fact, it can be said that her politics finally had less than selfish reasoning. Previously, she had fought a fight for her own personal agenda more than anything in order to create space for her own eclecticism; however, after the war, new meaning could be found within her. Based on her political and fictional writing, the war became essential in shaping her growth.

The author's works often dulled out, which meant she had to stay relevant in the period Augusta Fink calls "The Dazzle of New York," which started in 1906 and continued well into the 1920s.[108] In this period, Austin published and re-published works such as *The Man Jesus* (1925), *Starry Adventure* (1931), and *One Smoke Stories* (1934), as well as nonfiction such as *The American Rhythm: Studies and Re-expressions of American Songs* (1923), *Everyman's Genius* (1925), *Taos Pueblo* (1930), and *Earth Horizon* (1932). The amount of published works, which includes many more titles than those listed here, leads to the understanding that she continued to be efficient until the end of her life. However, it also shows that she was dependent on producing as her works were

---

[105] Austin, *Earth Horizon*, 127-129, 325-329, 398.
[106] Ibid., 227-229.
[107] Ibid., 114
[108] Fink, *I-Mary*, 177.

often only interesting for so long before they were forgotten, and thus she had to continue to produce in order to remain relevant and earn money.

Austin went through life in a somewhat nomadic manner. She traveled between states and cities and toured as a lecturer while also writing and continuing her activism, and her ways of being tremendously varied, to the point of being too many, were enhanced in New York because the arena kept humming to her beat, and she did the same in her continuous search for the development of reforms. After the death of her daughter Ruth on 13 November 1918, Austin was left in a state of deep sorrow that needed to be lived through; it was heartbreak all over again, which only time could mend.

In the year 1919, the author sold her last property in Carmel, however her roots in the West never fully took hold, and she continued to go back and forth between the East and the West. In the summer of 1922 she returned to Carmel, which it is claimed brought her happiness again, thus the years between 1920 and 1924 were her years in the West.[109] Austin's diversity continued well after the war, and it is evident in her writing and actions that she thought there might be a pronounced deal to get out of being a woman. What we see is her need to continue expanding her relevance because she was not done saying what she had to say.

This new phase of her life was filled with new confidence, exemplarily in an instance where George Bernard Shaw was intrigued by her.[110] Comically enough, Austin herself is quoted as saying, with regard to her romantic relationships, "All I can say is that if I had had as much attention when I was in my twenties or thirties as I am having in my fifties, it would have ruined me," however she valued all of her acquaintances (and the attention she got) highly and equally.[111] The author was productive, as well as much wiser, in the period after the war, as she continued what had been started during the war, but in a calmer manner; she kept seeking a place for herself in a more permanent approach, as she did not want her works to die out too soon (as they so often did after they were published) in the rebuilding phases after the war and the associated new social structures.

Susan Goodman and Carl Dawson dedicate a whole chapter in *Mary Austin and the American West* to the importance of her New York years after 1920, because the years after the war were a time of many shifts for Austin's persona

---

[109] Ibid., 206.
[110] Ibid., 199.
[111] Goodman and Dawson, *Mary Austin and the American West*, 200.

and perceptions of her, and she was also established within intellectual circles and as a notable person.

The author was in a new era of confidence, perhaps because of the emancipation of women as well all the newfound personal support she was getting. She continued to explore her craft, and it was through criticism and praise that she stayed "true to her talents."[112] The public was more into her mellower journalism, which needed to be done for the sake of an income, however she still spoke out on topics of politics, birth control, religion, theater, etc. One of the most important things she did in the period after the war was lecturing in the years between 1922 and 1931.[113] In the 1920s she was also a member of the Society of Women Geographers, and perhaps her vast interest in the subject grew because of the encouragements of and the shared interests with her friend, and many assumed lover, the ecologist Daniel T. MacDougal (1865-1958), who worked at the University of Arizona.[114] MacDougal had an intimate relationship with Austin in the years after the First World War.[115] Her developing interest in more practical geography most likely stems from her long relationship with nature, flora and fauna, and a love of the West. Because Austin had a special love for MacDougal, his ideas in his letters, in which he described the Arizona desert to Austin and suggested that

---

[112] Ibid., 201-202.
[113] Ibid., 206-207. Her lectures include those that took place at Carmel; New York; the University of California, Berkeley (five times in 1922 and for several years in the summer school on American rhythm and theater); Monterey (on patterns of American literature); Cincinnati (on the poetry of Native Americans); Boston (on community culture and psychology); Elizabeth, New Jersey; Clark University (on spiritualism and death); Fort Worth (on American rhythm); Dallas (on the shape of society); Evanston (on Iowa); Carlinville, Illinois; the University of California, Los Angeles (five lectures on American literature); Chicago (on Native Americans); Boston again (on religion); Philadelphia; Seattle; Waterbury, Connecticut; Memphis; the Denver Writers' Colony; England (at the Fabian Summer School); Providence, Rhode Island (on the American pattern); Kansas City; St. Louis; and Keene, New Hampshire (on social patterns of the American novel). She also lectured in Santa Fe (on colonial arts) and Taos (on southwestern literature and the common life).
[114] Sharon E. Kingsland, "The Battling Botanist: Daniel Trembly MacDougal, Mutation Theory, and the Rise of Experimental Evolutionary Biology in America, 1900-1912," *Isis* 82, no. 3 (1991): 479-509.
[115] For further reading on this topic, see Goodman and Dawson, *Mary Austin and the American West*.

she orient herself with nature by looking at maps,[116] was another thing that contributed to Austin's love for Western landscapes.

The confidence in her female empowerment advocacy was evident in how she promoted non-traditional gender roles and family structures, more than anything else, with a grander purpose than previously, such as in an article published in 1922 titled "Wife right 'Boss,' Novelist Believes."[117] In this article, Austin is quoted as saying that the American home had failed and that "family life is not what it used to be" because "it has failed to be the center of culture and intellectual interest."[118]

Her circle of friendship extended to other figures who were also against the nuclear family structure, such as Charlotte Perkins Gilman, Emma Goldman, etc. Goldman, for example, wrote in 1911:

> ...time and again it has been conclusively proved that the old matrimonial relation restricted woman to the function of man's servant and the bearer of his children. And yet we find many emancipated women who prefer marriage, with all its deficiencies, to the narrowness of an unmarried life: narrow and unendurable because of the chains of moral and social prejudice that cramp and bind her nature.[119]

These ideas naturally affected and transformed Austin, and she turned into her own woman as time went by and as a result of the global situation around her, as well as the new conditions of the post-war times. Those speeches that she had previously made now made sense because they fit into the time. Texts such as those of Goldman and Gilman were inspirational for Austin, who recognized the importance of the war as another step toward emancipation, which is evident in her 1918 work "Sex Emancipation Through War."[120] In this essay, Austin demonstrates how the participation of women in the war effort enhanced the process of expanding female influence in American public life.[121] Austin, at times mellow, was political in all the right ways during the

---

[116] Daniel T. MacDougal, 5 April 1920, in the Mary Austin Papers, Huntington Library. In this passage, MacDougal refers to Carl Lumholtz's *New Trails in Mexico* (Scribners, 1912), which was reprinted by the University of Arizona Press in 1990, and W. J. McGee, "The Old Yuma Trail," *National Geographic* (March-April 1901).

[117] Mary Austin, "Wife right 'Boss,' Novelist Believes," *The Washington Herald*, December 9, 1922, 5.

[118] Ibid.

[119] Goldman, *Anarchism and Other Essays*, 219-231.

[120] Austin, *Beyond Borders*, 44-54.

[121] Ibid., 43.

First World War, and it was the reception of this exact reaction that later helped the foundation of the rebellion against the systematic oppression of women based on uneven gender distribution and patriarchal dominance.

The use of literature by intellectuals such as Austin and those who were like-minded to her politics took a great leap as a result of the war, and it was this that continued afterward.[122] However, the likes of Gilman and Austin still had a fundamental belief in tradition despite their wish for emancipation. *The Young Woman Citizen* was only one of many works meant to prepare women, the non-participant sex, to own up to their right of citizenship.[123] This was a moment in which the contemporary perception was that women were not writing "crappy stuff anymore."[124]

Direct connections between Austin and these contemporary women are significant because American feminists in the second wave draw on their connections and intellectual inspirations gained from each other as exemplary models to follow as feminists in their sisterhood. It was in her radicalization with like-minded women that this 'no-nonsense attitude' continued to flourish with her wider circle of like-minded women, such as Elizabeth Gurley Flynn (1890-1964), who greatly admired *A Woman of Genius*, or Margaret Sanger (1879-1966), a great advocate of sexual education. Austin admired the fearlessness in Sanger as a woman of courage and force. The list of notable names continues and, as previously mentioned, also includes Charlotte Perkins Gilman, described as Herbert Hoover's (1874-1964) nightmare as well as "the most intransigent feminist of them all, the one most exclusively concerned with the improvement of the lot of woman, the least likely to compromise at the instance of man, child, church, state, or devil."[125]

There was also Emma Goldman, who has been credited as a woman who established love as a serious topic.[126] Perhaps above all else, "life in the Village meant meeting and accepting people of differing professions, persuasions, sexual orientations, politics, and ambitions; and Austin found these in spades at Mabel Dodge's evenings."[127] The Village was where such freedom of expression was welcomed, and it can be seen as the embodiment of a direct contrast to the wider United States. The Village was a place where the

---

[122] Gabrielson, "Woman-Thought," 651.
[123] Ibid., 652.
[124] "Bookdom," *The Washington Herald*, January 5, 1919, 6.
[125] Floyd Dell, *Women as World Builders: Studies in Modern Feminism* (Chicago: Forbes and Company, 1913), 22.
[126] Goodman and Dawson, *Mary Austin and the American West*, 159.
[127] Ibid., 173.

expression of one's place, belonging, identity, and citizenship was fluid and tolerant: "an alternative society," as scholar Ross J. Wilson describes it.[128]

The reception of radical ideas after the war was apparent, for example, in the statement that "Twenty-Six Jayne Street by Mary Austin is a tale of radical thinkers, artists and social reformers who lead the well-press-agented life of Greenwich Village."[129] The idea that both Austin and her work were marked as radical is the triumph to take away from this. Perhaps this deep reliability which the author got was from the authority she showed in her fight for both women as well as Native Americans; for instance, in 1926, she was referred to as a spokesperson for Indians in Santa Fe.[130] This is easily linked to the era that Augusta Fink refers to as "Santa Fe: Home to Her Heartland."[131]

However, what we see the most appreciation for is the continuous praise for her works related to emancipation, the key work here being *The Young Woman Citizen*, because, as previously mentioned, it was valued with new perceptiveness after the war was over and society had to reconsider itself,[132] and "books for women voters" now got more space to flourish.[133] The teaching of how to take ownership of one's citizenship is perhaps feminist in contemporary thought, but it was a matter of practicality at that point.

Feminism, during and after the First World War (having been developing beforehand), as portrayed by Austin, was in many ways a journey: it was a cry for emancipation and to get away from imbalances based on gender in political rights above all else, and then grew during the global conflict because the men were at the front, before it got stronger immediately after the war when it justifiably became modern feminism because of the rebuilding that was necessary. In *The Legacy of Second-Wave Feminism in American Politics* (2018), edited by Angie Maxwell and Todd Shields, one can read about the second wave, which drew inspiration from this first wave of political women to mark themselves on the economic, political, and social landscape, who came under attack for faults in their wave, e.g. the second wave's exclusion of marginalized groups, such as African American women and lesbians. The reason why this particular discussion is interesting is because the universal idea is that feminism means inclusion for all, because the goal (in this case in

---

[128] Wilson, *New York and the First World War*, 19.
[129] "Tabloid Book Reviews," *The Seattle Star*, July 26, 1920, 9.
[130] "Mary Austin in List," *The Evening Star*, October 6, 1926, 10.
[131] Fink, *I-Mary*, 223.
[132] "Books added to Public Library," *Arizona Republican*, August 4, 1929, 3; "Good Old Summertime," *The Glasgow Courier*, July 2, 1920, 2.
[133] "Books for Women Voters," *Evening Times*, February 10, 1920, 9.

the US) is to influence the economy and theology, to partake in political activism as equals, and to affect electoral success, attitudes toward homosexuality, the support of gay marriage, etc. Yet, in many ways, this was reserved for white upper-class women once again because of the (unintentional) exclusion of the various sidelined groups.

When exploring the topics of women's emancipation as portrayed in Austin's works, as well as those of Gilman, Goldman, etc., the topics of feminism and spirituality come up in a way that explains the two are much more in parallel than one would assume, at least the so-called radical aspects, which in reality are not so radical. It can be said that devotion in beliefs is perhaps more about commitment and faith: the commitment to feminism, the commitment to God, etc.

In *Earth Horizon*, Austin reports mystical experiences with God and nature that made her feel there was a particular pattern to her existence, a pattern that would make its shape known to her over the years in many forms, but most importantly of all she says, "it is not that we work upon the Cosmos, but it works in us."[134] Statements such as this are what create the main binding agent for all the different ways in which the author explored religion on a personal level, but also in her writing. Alongside *Christ in Italy* and her next religious writing, *The Man Jesus: Being a Brief Account of the Life and Teachings of the Prophet of Nazareth*, which was published in 1915 (and then re-published several times), is one of her most significant books, *The Ford* (1918). I have focused on the feminist and impact of war aspects of this book above, however many religious notions are also present. *The Ford* is not specifically a Christian book, but nevertheless it is filled with spiritual connections, which in many ways reflect the writer in general, whether it be Native American spirituality or Christianity. Many writers have looked into this matter, such as John Peterson in "Wrestling with 'Half Gods': Biblical Discourse in Mary Austin's The Ford,"[135] which goes into the Christian aspects of the book. Perhaps one of the most illuminating cross-comparison works is *Dancing Ghosts: Native American and Christian Syncretism in Mary Austin's Work* (1998) by Mark T. Hoyer.

Dr. Gina Messina-Dysert, who is the Dean of the School of Graduate and Professional Studies at the Ursuline College, Ohio, and co-founder of the website *Feminism and Religion*, argued in a lecture on "The new feminist revolution in religion" that the basis of the first wave of feminism was indeed

---

[134] Austin, *Earth Horizon*, 368.
[135] John Peterson, "Wrestling with 'Half Gods': Biblical Discourse in Mary Austin's *The Ford*," *Christianity & Literature* 67, no. 4 (2018): 653-668.

built on Christian values, as it was a large social reform effort that drew on regular people's lives. Sandra Adickes describes these trying times as optimistic and states that war and new thoughts led to the birth of a new spirit,[136] which she describes as a "religion without a name." Often, religion is the foundation for the oppression of many women, and existing in its patriarchal structure proves difficult for countless people, among whom are Austin and women like her who wished to exist within both realms, on the basis of arguments such as how religion was more organized in areas where politics was lacking and how this was benefiting 'bad people' in the social revolution in America. Simply put, feminism is the extermination of all oppressions and recognizes that in order to fight such injustice, all 'isms' – racism, classism, heterosexism, sexism, etc. – had to be fought wherever they were, even in religious arenas.

Writing was what created a direct line between the many sides of the author; it gave her independence from herself, as well as from the world around her, which included her upbringing and family. She reached an all-time high in demanding equal political rights during the war period, however it was in the aftermath of the war and in her spirituality that she found more meaning in why she wrote as she did because others finally gave meaning to her writing. The building of identity for herself and others, as a result of the war, was the biggest motive to continue her writing, activism, and constant intellectual development. In *Remembering War: The Great War Between Memory and History in the Twentieth Century* (2006), Jay Winter writes about soldier's tales: about memories and identities, shell shock, and post-war mentalities. The idea is that the Great War reconfigured popular and medical notions about memory.[137] Women did not go to the front, but they were involved on the home front; this participation in society is what the new wave of feminist identity built on. The creation of memory about how much women contributed, and the feminist value in that, is what the post-war perception ultimately was.

The reception of her work by the second wave of American feminists of the 1960s and 1970s was therefore just another stone in the road toward the creation of a feminist identity. The fact that the likes of Austin were active in critical times served as a motivation when women were fighting for their social rights. They were feminist, however the inquiry of whether the term 'feminist' is appropriate to describe the thoughts and actions of women in

---

[136] Adickes, *To Be Young Was Very Heaven*, 3.
[137] Jay Winter, *Remembering War: The Great War Between Memory and History in the Twentieth Century* (New Haven, CT: Yale University Press, 2006), 52-55.

other times and places is not a simple matter of definition because it is subjective to the time, and the term has also changed significantly since its 'birth.' Changes have also occurred within our understanding of what constitutes gender; thus, different forms of feminism have different understandings of gender. However, it is at the foundation of feminism, where gender itself cannot be separated from factors such as race, class, sexual identity, etc., where the neglect of other groups happens.[138]

It cannot be claimed that the second wave of white feminists in America truly took up the fight for women of color because their fight went in parallel with the civil rights movement for a few years (until the late 1960s), and thus someone had to be forgotten: women of color. Austin's legacy in fighting for the rights of Native Americans, especially Native American women, is not something we see projected strongly in the second wave of feminism, perhaps because they did not prioritize minorities. In this regard, we can determine certain attributes were lacking in the fight for all, and therefore there is also reason to question the reception and recreation of history.

In her article "Two Feminist Views on the Self, Identity and Collective Action," Margaret A. McLaren explores the creation of feminist identity building, which evidentially is what this entire book is trying to pinpoint through the study of Austin's contribution to the construction of a feminist identity.[139] The building of a feminist identity, collectively or individually, has its own set of values and research, and McLaren takes a close look at the importance of building a feminist identity by comparing two significant works: Allison Weir's *Sacrificial Logics: Feminist Theory and the Critique of Identity* and *Feminisms and the Self: The Web of Identity* by Morwenna Griffiths.[140] The cross-comparison provides useful theoretical ground for understanding the different factors that come into play in the creation of such an identity (regardless of time and space). Weir argues that identity is negative as repression, exclusion, or domination. The positive is in correcting the overemphasis on separation that is seen as the normative ideal for (male) identity, while feminists posit a relational identity, which accepts that

---

[138] Kamala Visweswaran, "Histories of Feminist Ethnography," *Annual Review of Anthropology* 26 (1997): 591-592.
[139] McLaren, "Two Feminist Views on the Self," 120-125.
[140] Morwenna Griffiths, *Feminisms and the Self: The Web of Identity* (New York: Routledge, 1996); Allison Weir, *Sacrificial Logics: Feminist Theory and the Critique of Identity* (New York: Routledge, 1996).

separation equals domination.[141] The idea of a negative logic of identity sacrifice (regarding gender) excludes difference (intersectionality?).

While Weir argues that the attempt to reconcile differences and contradictions in one's own identity is essential to self-identity, Griffiths' approach seeks a more general approach (much like her entire book); self-identity is a web that is constructed out of interactions, e.g. radical women's interactions with each other as a further development of their already-established self-identity through the process of elimination.[142] The establishment of the identity of the individuals of the first wave became the building blocks of the second wave in order for them to take collective action, which they had witnessed in the previous generation of pioneering women.

On the subject of the feminist wave, Austin disliked the concept of 'isms,' and thus she was somewhat imprecise in her standpoints, for example in the concept of how she worked for feminist causes but not for feminism, as it was in its developmental phase. It is fair to note that feminism was still in its infancy, and the vocabulary and experience of what it was at the time were not yet in place; thus, the association with a 'bad ism' might have been what made Austin dismiss the movement. However, the root was that she believed that nobody, regardless of gender, had any moral superiority. Sure enough, she fought for equality, but it was on the basis of fairness, as she – like the patriarchy – did not believe that absolute empowerment guaranteed a better world. Women, much like men, should have the same rights because whether the world is better or worse can hardly be decided on the basis of gender, as one or the other was likely to mess it up in any case.

In 1927, she once again discussed this matter publicly in an article, in which she said:

> Too much has been made of the long rankling injustice of woman's position in the nineteenth century and earlier. Too little of that injustice was intended as such or can be historically traced to male initiative, to have become legitimately the source of widespread resentment. What every honest feminist now knows is that they simply seized upon existing injustices, sought them out, and flourished them as so many excuses for entitling them to what they so ardently wanted, a working partnership in social affairs.[143]

---

[141] McLaren, "Two Feminist Views on the Self," 120.
[142] Ibid., 122-125.
[143] Goodman and Dawson, *Mary Austin and the American West*, 171-172.

It is on the basis of the continuous demand for equal partnership that we realize why she never took a drastic stand with radical feminists, even though we color her as one: she wanted to keep her agenda going, but also to be tolerated by the masses (both men and women). This eclectic behavior is what kept her going for so long, because she continuously got along with everyone. This is evident in newspapers and other mentions of her, but also in a comparison of her with Emma Goldman, who was seen as 'dangerous' by Hoover, whereas Austin was his friend. This goes to show that she was eager to please, despite also wanting to make a change.

On the other hand, the American critic and biographer Carl Van Doren (1885-1950) wrote in *Contemporary American Novelists* (1922) that "she herself prefers less to be judged by any of her numerous books ... than to be regarded as a figure laboring somewhat anonymously toward the development of a national culture founded at all points on national realities."[144] Van Doren's admiration for Austin leads him to see her much as she saw herself through those New York years: courageous, ambitious, but struggling between the talented writer and the eclectic expert on all things, which in many ways shows that, much like everyone else, Austin wished to control how she was perceived. She was radical enough to be interesting but mellow enough not to be an object of too much personal rage or "a dangerous woman" like other radical icons.

The poet Floyd Dell (1887-1969) wrote that Greenwich Village offered a "moral health resort where people came to solve some of their life problems,"[145] because there were many characters similar to Austin, not only the previously mentioned radical women but also others who were similar in their specific personal traits, like those who were passionate about the West, e.g. Mabel Dodge (1879-1962). Dodge was continuously chasing whatever was new and exciting for her own self, which is what Austin was also doing in all of her contributions. Whatever one's motive for being there, life in the Village meant meeting and accepting people different from oneself, but who were

---

[144] Catrin Gersdorf, *The Poetics and Politics of the Desert Landscape and the Construction of America* (New York: Rodopi, 2009), 239: Carl van Doren, *Contemporary American Novelists (1900-1920)* (Salt Lake City, UT: Project Gutenberg Literary Archive Foundation, 2009).
[145] Floyd Dell, *Homecoming: An Autobiography* (New York: Farrar & Rinehart, 1933), 272; Kenneth S. Lynn, "The Rebels of Greenwich Village," *Perspectives in American History* 8 (1974): 335-380.

also similar in many ways. Austin found someone who was "different but similar" in Dodge.[146]

Melody Graulich writes in her afterword in the 1991 edition of *Earth Horizon* that by the time the forty-six-year-old Austin wrote her autobiography, she was well aware that she had left her mark on American literature and culture and was deservedly proud of her accomplishments and achievements. Her versatility and energy are evident in the long list of what she produced and in looking at who she started out as and who she became, as well as her friendships and acquaintances.[147] The 're-discovering' of her writing was of no surprise, as it had previously been predicted that she was "a 'future' person – one who will, a century from now, appear as a writer of major stature in the complex matrix of our American culture."[148]

Upon closer inspection, what feminism meant in the US context before the war, how a shift took place with the war and the new gender roles and social structures, and how these new roles affected the relationship between men and women after the war have now been established. The bitterness of men that is evident in the literature, as well as the empowerment of women, is unmistakable in US politics, and parallels have been drawn with how Austin fitted into the bigger picture during and after the war, as a result of who she was prior to it.

The power of the reception of her work by the second wave is something that had long been predicted (Ansel Adams), and the second wave's eclecticism matched Austin's own. The need to be valued corresponded culturally with the identity building and wishes of the modern feminists of the 1960s and 1970s.[149] The building of identity is done collectively, and by relating to the author and like-minded women's 'radical mindset' for their time, it was much easier to justify their contemporary radicalism because so many had successfully rebelled before them. There is evidence of intersectionality within Greenwich

---

[146] Mabel Dodge Luhan, *Movers and Shakers* (Albuquerque: University of New Mexico Press, 1985), 88.
[147] See previously mentioned names, e.g. Carl van Doren, Van Wyck Brooks (1886-1963), Willa Cather (1873-1947), Jack London, Vachel Lindsay, Charlotte Perkins Gilman, Herbert Hoover, Lincoln Steffens, Emma Goldman, Mabel Dodge Luhan, etc.
[148] Ansel Adams, "Notes to Mary Austin," in *Mary Hunter Austin: A Centennial Booklet Published by the Mary Austin Home* (Independence, CA: Mary Austin Home, 1968), 7.
[149] For further reading on the second wave of feminism in America, see Angie Maxwell and Todd Shields, *The Legacy of Second-Wave Feminism in American Politics* (Cham: Springer, 2018).

Village,[150] and although the term is modern, the ideas that the author built on qualify for the modern concept. Additionally, on one last post-war era note, it can be said that she was indeed feminist, but only insofar as the development of feminism was happening at the time, because feminism then was not necessarily the same as we define it today.

Like most artists, the author's journey was selfish because all of her books reflected something personal. *A Woman of Genius* attempted to clear her pains and emotion while her autobiography was also written in the same person, and the process of dealing with one's own emotional baggage more or less became the legacy of a whole generation. The naked truth required courage to "shear off what is not worthwhile."[151] It was in this naked truth that modern feminists found their identity, particularly scholars who could relate to it, such as Adrienne Rich, who in 1976 said that "the most notable fact that culture imprints on women is the sense of our limits."[152]

The public perception of Austin after the First World War varied, because as much as the author was celebrated as special in the aftermath, the contemporary sources mention her less and less frequently, as her radical relevance was now a shaky foundation that varied from period to period depending on what project was occupying her (teaching, touring, theater, etc. – whatever paid the bills). In 1926, *The Evening Star* (Washington) wrote that "Mary Austin of Santa Fe. N. Mex., foremost authority on the Pueblo Indians, is an active member of the new society and so, too, is the popular novelist Rose Wilder Lane, who has temporarily deserted fiction to study the fascinating history of Albania, past and present."[153] In 1929, *The Children Sing in the Far West* was published by Houghton Mifflin Co. The author is cited as saying that the book is a collective effort in which children helped make the songs. This book again shows the author going back to her interests in the West, as the songs are said to be Native-inspired.[154]

---

[150] Intersectionality refers to the cross-connections between categories such as race, class, and gender when applied to individuals or groups to better understand the creation of overlapping and interdependent systems of discrimination or disadvantage. Although this intersectionality is present in Austin, it is lacking from the second wave's inclusion of women of color.
[151] Austin, *Earth Horizon*, 384.
[152] Ibid., 392 (see also for similar ideas by other intellectuals sparked by Austin).
[153] "Mary Austin in List," *The Evening Star*, October 6, 1926, 10.
[154] "The Children Sing In The Far West. Mary Austin. Houghton Mifflin Co," *The Evening Star*, January 15, 1929, 8.

Related to matters of education, which can be linked to the taxing time in the author's life when she was touring and lecturing, in April of 1931, *The Evening Star* once again reported news about her. This time, it was on how "US Education Head Leaves on Long Tour," and it spoke about inspection trips that would stretch to places from Alaska to Mexico City, and it is in connection with the latter that Mary Austin appears: "the sixth annual seminar [is to be] conducted by the Committee on Cultural Relations With Latin America at Mexico City July 4 to 24. Seminar speakers from the United States will include Senator Dwight W. Morrow, Paul U. Kellogg, Judge Florence E. Allen and Mrs. Mary Austin."[155]

One article that might perhaps be rather political in today's society with the movement of self-aware and intelligent youth is the injustice of Thanksgiving, which many consider a violation against the Native Americans by the first settlers. A question thus arises in the article "It's Time to Talk Turkey" from 1932, which discusses the preparation of Thanksgiving turkey and President Hoover's message about its preparation. It is on the basis of this that Austin is quoted as saying that "Our elevation of the turkey to the place of honor on the Thanksgiving dinner table is not entirely owing to its traditional importance to the first American Thanksgiving day; it is a tribute to the homemaking instinct of the Puritan women who made the turkey brood a part of that association of men and their wild brethren which is inseparable from the human idea of home. The Indians domesticated the turkey chiefly for his feathers, which they prized. But I have no doubt that the English housewife, arriving chickenless, got her first feeling of being at home from the brooding cluck of the turkey hen about her door."[156] What is to be taken away from this article is the fact that the author's friendships continued to benefit her, such as the one with Hoover, as well as that she was still consulted about matters regarding Native Americans. The article is an example of what she called "a glitter piece," however, its significance in showing the essence of who Mary Hunter Austin continued to be is evident.[157]

Subsequent mentions of her were few and far between, and their significance varied; for instance, the review for *Earth Horizon* in the *Evening Star* in 1932 did not give any significant ideas other than the fact that Austin's autobiography would be presented with a review by Mrs. Helen Taylor Steinbarger.[158] Among the problematic elements we see in the newspapers'

---

[155] "US Education Head Leaves on Long Tour," *The Evening Star*, April 22, 1931, A-10.
[156] "It's Time to Talk Turkey," *Midland Journal*, November 11, 1932, 7.
[157] Ibid.
[158] "Plans Book Review," *The Evening Star*, November 29, 1932, b-5.

mentions of her, of which there are several hundred, though the majority are only in quick passing, is the fact that it is often the same news source, which might lead us to doubt their credibility, as one wonders why some newspapers in particular chose to include her while others did not. Was it her friendship with journalists? Her political values or simply the long relationship with the war period when the author was significant were often reported on, and thus loyalty to her intellect continued long after her personal peak. Regardless of this concern, Austin's moves back and forth to the West allowed her to regain some of her significance in the media of the West; for example, *The Border Vidette* (Santa Cruz) reported that "an author in the current issue of Nation, Mary Austin, describes one of these present-day characters as, 'Americans We Like, Hunt of Arizona,' where Austin can be read supporting Governor George Hunt as an outstanding guy and candidate for the state's best. The article concludes with the fact that, 'in part this may be owing to the fact that Arizona is still close enough to pioneer conditions to constitute Hunt's particular personal qualities—courage, honesty and self-direction,'"[159] in reference to the fact that he had all the good qualities and an abundance of wealth. What can be gathered from this article is Austin's endorsement of male politicians, which is without any need to overstep any boundaries or raise any questions regarding gender or political ideologies, but rather which only contains good character traits such as "courage, honesty and self-direction" – all positive attributes that Austin evidently wished to possess herself. It also displays her growth, as one detects less anger in contrast to what she expressed and wrote in times of war and distress (e.g. "Sex Emancipation Through War"); there is no anger about men's sutured bursting of/by sex and her belief that men's extinction of masculinity ran aimlessly and chaotically.[160]

In later years, the mentions of Austin were less than impressive in the media, and more mentions are available in her personal correspondence. However, what we can gather from this is that her role in the Village no longer made her visible in the press alongside other profiled people. The brief mentions every now and then were about other subjects instead of the common supportive role at "luncheons" or "suffrage rallies," where her name had been mentioned in passing alongside many others, which evidently occurred in the earlier years when she was in more directly radical circles.

The birth of modern media had its high-tide during the war, and the influence of the war obviously affected the fact that an activist such as Austin

---

[159] "Arizona's Transition Period," *The Border Vidette*, January 12, 1929, no. 2; see also in the *Arizona Star* of the same date.
[160] Austin, *Beyond Borders*, 44.

was highly visible when directly linked to war and women's causes, as well as in the first couple of years after its end while her activism was contributing to the rebuilding of society (citizenship, emancipation, etc.). However, after the war, with the narrative of Austin not being too politically driven in parallel to the war, she was less of a priority, and the economic boom of journalism and newspapers also created a sea in which one could easily get lost. A greater change can be seen in the fact that she was now evolving more personally than publicly.

Chapter 2
The Impact of World War One

Books on the First World War are legion, and the centennial created further intensified interest in the events between 1914 and 1918, including works on New York City.¹ This chapter will show how the war influenced Mary Hunter Austin while she stayed in the metropolis in these years, as well as the overall climate in the city as an effect of the war. The history of the war and the perspectives of historians have shifted in the last decades, not only in the case of WWI but within a wider movement in history, away from stories about decisive battles and great men, be they politicians or generals, to look at ordinary women and men and how their lives were changed by the war and its impact.² This chapter does not provide a linear approach to events but presents a discussion around the changes caused by the war.

Although it was not the first of its kind, as European powers had been fighting among themselves endlessly for hundreds of years, the conflict expanded to involve the entirety of the globe.³ The United States wished to remain neutral and stayed as such until 1917. On 14 October, President Woodrow Wilson (1856-1924) rejected Germany's request for a peace dialog, and on 1 November, the United States Army marched into final advance, which resulted in Germany

---

¹ For further reading on the topic of World War I in the US and New York, see Adickes, *To Be Young Was Very Heaven*; Kennedy, *Over Here*; Wilson, *New York and the First World War*. Broader works on the impact of war on American society include, among others, Lawrence Freedman, *War* (New York: Oxford University Press, 1994); Ross Gregory, *The Origins of American Intervention in the First World War* (New York: Norton & Company, Inc., 1972); G. J. Meyer, *The World Remade America in World War I* (New York: Bantam Books, 2016); Anne Cipriano Venzon, ed., *The United States in the First World War: An Encyclopedia* (New York: Routledge, 2012); Robert H. Zieger, *America's Great War: World War I and the American Experience* (New York: Rowman & Littlefield Publishers, Inc., 2001).
² George Robb and W. Brian Newsome, "Introduction: Rethinking World War I: Occupation, Liberation, and Reconstruction," *Economic and Political Weekly* 3, no. 35 (August-September 2010): 50-57.
³ Michael Howard, *The First World War: A Very Short Introduction* (New York: Oxford University Press, 2002), 1-14. For further reading, see Wilson, *New York and the First World War*, 41-80.

requesting a truce on 6 November.[4] WWI had extensive political, economic, and cultural significance for New York, Mary Hunter Austin, and the world in general. The powers of Russia, Germany, Austria-Hungary, and the Ottoman Empire collapsed in part as a result of the war and new states being established. The war led to the flourishment of extreme ideologies such as fascism, Nazism, communism, etc., which in turn was the gateway to the Second World War. A positive impact from the war, however, was women in America mobilizing for the right to vote and to take a role that was greater than the domestic one they had had before the war. It allowed the independence ideas of individuals such as Austin to blossom, and her stance on not being limited as a woman was free to roam in the chaotic conditions caused by the war. Artists such as her got the arena to have an impact beyond what they had previously had simply through their art because they now had new credibility for their political thoughts, including because this war was inclusive of pluralities of genders, nations, social classes, and roles.

In the early twentieth century, the ideas that "bad states" waged wars while "good states" coexisted in peace and harmony gained momentum, which is a narrative often seen in both the propaganda of the Wilson administration and in Austin's work, as she urges women not to be passive because America needs them.[5]

With the numerous universal ideologies battling for sovereignty, e.g. liberalism, fascism, communism, etc., the great powers such as the United States saw themselves as champions of peaceful aggressors and not at all as problematic themselves. The idea of "a war to end all wars" and the justification which President Wilson gave to the United States' entrance into it was because of the nation's implementation of a moral obligation to help the forces of light – the democratic states – in their struggles against the forces of darkness – the authoritarian states.[6]

Socialists condemn war because they see it as brutal and uncalled for, as they believe that war is directly connected to social classes – and war can only be abolished if social classes are as well, e.g. in addition to a war such as WWI, there is also the war between wage-workers and the upper-class bourgeoise.[7]

---

[4] Sue Vander Hook, *The United States Enters World War I* (Minnesota: Abdo Publishing, 2010), 98.
[5] Close readings of Austin's texts such as "Sex Emancipation Through War" and *The Young Woman Citizen* will provide more detailed explanations for this statement.
[6] Freedman, *War*, 67-68.
[7] Ibid., 95.

Some argue that women have "a certain luxury in being the outsiders" in war because they were not directly involved and, thus, have no responsibility for it.[8] However, based on what we see in the sources of females' activity in war (e.g. serving at the frontline and those who were home-based) and the social changes after the war, this statement is to be argued against.[9]

The mainstream American savior idea, and one which President Wilson was not alone in thinking, was that this was the war to end all wars. F. Scott Fitzgerald (1896-1940) wrote that "no European will ever do that again in this generation"[10] in reference to how the slow march of the British in battle across dead bodies was enough trauma for a lifetime. The onset of the First World War and its brutality was shocking to the point that Durkheim himself existed in disbelief when having to account for this "historical glitch," and he utilized his solidarity argument that the Great War was a temporary pathological state, much like what we see American writers argue: humanity should not be capable of such evils in the long term because it goes against our very own human civilization.[11] WWI, despite (or because of) its violence, trauma, and shame, was part of the process of the modern world becoming what it is today, from infrastructures and the abolishment of superpowers to the development of new states.

Much like previous wars, Americans deemed WWI a European war. This book examines the impact of the war on Mary Hunter Austin, a period in which she was residing in New York City, and thus the place becomes an important factor. Just as it looks at how the war impacted Austin, the book also looks at how the war impacted her country and city of residency in order to map out its influences on her. Politically, it is also essential to understand the activities of the military and the drive/passion of the common people and their efforts across all aspects of the war (e.g. not just military, but socially and so on). The

---

[8] Ibid., 132.
[9] For further reading on women's role in the war, see Chris Dubbs, *An Unladylike Profession: American Women War Correspondents in World War I* (Lincoln, NE: University of Nebraska Press, 2020); Lettie Gavin, *American Women In World War I: They Also Served* (Boulder, CO: University Press of Colorado, 2011); Dorothy Schneider and Carl J. Schneider, *Into the Breach: American Women Overseas in World War I* (New Zealand: Penguin Books, 1991).
[10] F. Scott Fitzgerald, *Tender Is the Night* (New York: Cambridge University Press, 2012), 67-68. For further reading from American literary figures who served in the war and later wrote about it, see Ernest Hemingway, *A Farewell to Arms: The Hemingway Library Edition* (New York: Scribner, 2014).
[11] Sinisa Malesevic, *Sociology of War and Violence* (New York: Cambridge University Press, 2010), 21.

human relationship with war and violence is a complex as well as paradoxical one because, in addition to the violent acts, there is the popular culture connotation that comes with war: its impacts, and thus transformations, on the social sphere.

The First World War, in addition to being the first heavily industrialized war, was also different because of its impact on literature, social systems, cultures, and religions, as well as its impact on the lives of those on the frontlines.[12] New York City went through what Ross J. Wilson calls "vast alterations in its governance,"[13] referring to the new way in which warfare was led at home through posters, newspapers, magazines, films, and the diaries and letters of ordinary soldiers and civilians, which is also the approach historians are taking.[14] Wilson argues that war was conducted not only on the battlefield but also in people's daily lives through the mass media.

War has been defined as an area of male dominance because the majority of military activities and decades of trench warfare have been defined and painted by the men on the frontline. Given this background to the popular narratives and definitions of war and violence, it is not strange that women at home were seen as being "safe and sound in their beds," with no further consideration for their ill-being at home, where they were balancing the social (economic and political) changes.[15] It was not so much in the collective self-awareness of the time that the war led to active social changes but more that changes were happening on the basis of practicality, and modern scholars have approaches that are giving new life to the impact of the war, e.g. looking at different groups such as the East Side Jewish Americans and stay-at-home mothers who could not afford basic food supplies. The rise in education for the average citizen increased questions about the regular man and woman on the street. The events which concerned strikes, labor shortages, women workers, rationing, food riots, and welfare policies are significant because they portray a picture of the importance of the average things in life.[16]

The physical and ideological transformation of New York during the war and the post-war period is evident in all things, and the war can be said to have

---

[12] Ibid.
[13] Wilson, *New York and The First World War*, 1.
[14] Ibid.
[15] Angela K. Smith, *The Second Battlefield: Women, Modernism and the First World War* (Manchester: Manchester University Press, 2000), 2-10. For further reading on women in the line of defense, see Catherine Marshall, *Militarism versus Feminism* (London: Virago, 1987).
[16] Robb and Newsome, "Introduction," 6.

truly made the place a metropolis, as it was the place where men and materials were sent out into the world.

WWI was a process that turned an immigrant metropolis into an American city. Wilson argues this was not just to reshape the place to fit authority and private business to fit the model of a uniform capitalist agenda, but also because immigrant groups themselves wished to be Americanized. Before the war, immigrants had seen themselves as American, and this process of becoming more so was welcome for many because it ensured that they actually fitted this profile, as the war served to integrate communities and shape the New York we know today.[17]

Lester Kurtz writes in the *Encyclopedia of Violence, Peace, and Conflict* about how conflict can be carried out in a variety of ways, from war and violence on one end of the spectrum to nonviolent struggle on the other. The meaning of violent conflict has changed immensely, and thus our approach to understanding it has as well.[18] The human relationship with violence and war is complex and paradoxical because we as humans condemn violent acts/the physical harm of others and control such behavior through legal systems, yet we have a long history of partaking in such events and have in modern times capitalized on the behaviors in the mass media which surrounds us despite advocating for peace.[19] This ultimately showcases the hypocritical behaviors of human beings, according to Malesevic, which can be linked to the hypocrisy of the American leadership in promising women and ethnic groups more than they ever intended to give them while using them as pawns in a violent world war.

In their 2017 article "Civil Society and Democracy in an Era of Inequality,"[20] Michael Bernhard, Tiago Fernandes, and Rui Branco argue that the adaptation of civil society to a radically changed environment affects different forms of inequality, which, in the case of WWI and civil unrest/contentment, fills most of the same criteria. The authors argue that with the rise of NGOs and the decline of traditional organizations such as unions, the impact of civil society has had a greater effect in reducing political and public inequalities than economic ones.[21] This idea can in theory be applied to the situation of WWI;

---

[17] Wilson, *New York and the First World War*, 218.
[18] Lester Kurtz, ed., *Encyclopedia of Violence, Peace, and Conflict* (Fairfax: Academic Press, 1999), 5.
[19] Malesevic, *Sociology of War and Violence*, 1.
[20] Michael Bernhard, Tiago Fernandes and Rui Branco, "Civil Society and Democracy in an Era of Inequality," *Comparative Politics* 49, no. 3 (2017): 297-309.
[21] Ibid., 302.

although women and ethnic groups lost their economic momentum after the war (despite being pledges in it), the effect it had on public and political inequality was unmatched because the imbalance became too great to remain unnoticed, leading to a long historical battle for change in various matters (e.g. women's right to vote and work and the civil rights movements).

America's neutrality plan did not last because the German powers continued their aggressive warfare, which included attacks on US ships.[22] In February 1917, the United States got ready for war after the reelection of President Wilson in 1916.[23] The country's late entrance left a lot of time for the United States to develop an overview of the situation, and many Americans (if not most) had the idea that they were aiding Europe in the war to end all wars but would not be involved themselves. Women in particular were strong war critics, as women at home historically did not benefit from wars, however this war was especially large in its scale: not only in its military, social, and political aspects but also the concomitant changes in gender roles, social classes, and the economic market.

The war's effect in New York specifically is of great significance as the city was and still is the melting pot of the world. The city was populated by people from all sorts of places; thus, there was no singular American identity, which is why the Americanization process was so important. The masses in New York were united by the place, but their ties to their original homelands, cultures, religions, etc. were still present, which in a way is what drove the place to become a metropolis, but this had to be neutralized along the way.[24] In the fifteen to twenty years prior to the war, the city had gone through a great population expansion at a rate of 3.20 percent, which was more than double or even triple that of places such as London and Paris.[25] Old buildings were being torn down to make way for new and improved ones, particularly apartment buildings to house the growing population of five million (1912).[26] Undoubtedly, one of the main reasons why Mary Hunter Austin and like-minded individuals thrived in New York was because of its unlimited opportunities for them to flourish in the urban space, as it became the center for the spirits of art, politics, and ideas. By the start of 1917, WWI had led to the loss of millions of lives, and although the United States had stayed neutral up until then, there were still propaganda

---

[22] John Merriman, *Modern Europe from the Renaissance to the Present* (New York: Yale University Press, 1996), 1072-1073.
[23] Ibid.
[24] Wilson, *New York and the First World War*, 34-35.
[25] Adickes, *To Be Young Was Very Heaven*, 12.
[26] Ibid.

campaigns that painted America as a savior. London kept the United States afloat with news that was carefully edited when it was not invented, but it was rarely identified as coming from official sources as most of it did not.[27] The fast flow of information in mass-print media allowed the nation to use the tension to promote why the world needed them so badly upon their entrance into the war. The war created the Americanization agenda, despite not giving anything back to many groups, thus minorities such as African Americans demonstrated through the use of silent parades or silent protests,[28] in which between 10,000-20,000 African American individuals walked silently with banners to demonstrate against the unfair expectation of them serving in the war when they had no civil rights or representations and were being directly harmed and hunted in the United States.[29]

Women and minorities, and minority women in particular, were in a position of disadvantage, making the city during the war a ticking timebomb, as the collection of domestic problems – among which were the expectations of sacrifice by minorities, ethnic groups, and women when the state gave them nothing in return – were used amidst the pressure of the war to create discussions and visibility. Allegiance to the principles of the United States was expected, yet the monetization of freedom of expression was flying high. The demand for a fight to ensure "democracy in the world" came at the cost of the United States oppressing its own citizens.[30] The metropolis went through a cleansing of removing the cultural and ethnic origins of businesses which had, previous to the war, been an important part of the city's economy and social groups, because ensuring that they were loyal to the flag was much more important than individual identity at a time of spectacular patriotism.[31]

Later on, the Selective Service Act hit New York harder than any other place in the United States as officials carried out a far greater organizational drive in the city.[32] The size of the place resulted in more eligible recruits and more draft boards, resulting in rising tensions because these boards demanded a big sacrifice from first- and second-generation immigrants, in whom there

---

[27] Meyer, *The World Remade America in World War I*, 178.
[28] Wilson, *New York and the First World War*, 169-170.
[29] Ibid.
[30] Ibid., 171-175.
[31] Ibid., 187. For further reading on the matter of 'Americanism,' see Kennedy, *Over Here*.
[32] The Selective Service Act was an act in which the federal government drafted men for army service through conscription. Emma Goldman was a strong opponent of conscription, resulting in the establishment of the No-Conscription League. For further reading, see Erika J. Pribanic-Smith and Jared Schroeder, *Emma Goldman's No-Conscription League and the First Amendment* (New York: Routledge, 2018).

was little trust to begin with, in the name of a united nation.[33] New York was a key place in military activities due to such events as the establishment of the 27th Division – one of the oldest organized military divisions in the United States, dating back to 1898, which was initially established as the New York branch of the National Guard.[34] As one can imagine, such an important military division in New York demonstrates how the city was transformed by the war. The division went through many re-organizations while mobilizing for the potential threat of war and then the war itself in 1917, and the last of its troops arrived back in New York and demobilized in March of 1919.[35]

There were additional enthusiastic responses among a majority of the metropolis' residents because this recruitment process was also a form of Americanization that had been developing in American institutions and society since 1914 when the war first broke out and people started to feel American, for better or worse.[36] Whilst this Americanization was good in some respects, it also showcased an exclusion of the universal identity of individuals/citizens.[37] Among the consequences that occurred because of the shaky trust in citizens, parallel to the expectation of their sacrifice and loyalty, was the 1917 Food Riots in the mainly Jewish community in Brooklyn. The riots soon spread, and women were on the frontlines.[38] The reason for the riots, and why women once again were affected and ready to fight, was because, upon America's entrance into the war, food prices had gone up 82 percent from the norm, leading to daily essentials such as butter and meat becoming luxury items that were hard to afford for the non-rich population (e.g. on the East Side). Cheese and potatoes, for instance, had increased in price by 100 percent, and plain flour was at its highest price since the Civil War.[39]

These are among the pointers to remember when we speak of women as the losers in war (which Austin spoke very actively on); in addition to being left alone to fend for themselves upon the men being recruited and sent away, women were left in an even harder situation with such flabbergasting prices.

---

[33] Wilson, *New York and the First World War*, 162.
[34] Venzon, *The United States in the First World War*, 636
[35] Ibid., 639. For further reading on the impact of troop settlements and mobilization's impact in New York, see Edward M. Coffman, *The War to End All Wars: The American Military Experience in World War I* (New York: Oxford University Press, 1986); Venzon, *The United States in the First World War*, 636-638, 664-666, 717.
[36] Wilson, *New York and the First World War*, 165.
[37] Ibid., 167.
[38] Mario Maffi, *Gateway to the Promised Land: Ethnic Cultures on New York's Lower East Side* (New York: New York University Press, 1995), 170-172.
[39] Ibid., 170.

Living situations were, thus, not only hard socially because of the distress of war but also financially because basic needs at home became impossible to keep up with for many. Because New York was such a haven for spirited artists, there was an increase in autobiographical fiction by individuals who came from more challenging backgrounds, as the role of memory became more and more decisive in writing, e.g. Austin's texts as a woman/disadvantaged female, or Jewish American authors who were at a disadvantage (because they were women and Jewish) as members of society, according to Mario Maffi's close readings of fiction of the time, such as *The Rise of David Levinsky* (1917) by the Jewish Lithuanian-American Abraham Cahan (1860-1951).[40] The correlations between fact and fiction presented by intellects such as Cahan and Austin, to name just two, truly showcased the social change in New York as a result of the war and which, as noted earlier in the chapter, became of greater interest in the 1960s, when it was given new life.

The physical and ideological transformation of the city, thanks to the war, made it more united, as the war had not only altered perceptions of who the aliens and the citizens were but also the essence of the city. To be honored as an American in New York City was a process that the post-war period showcased clearly through monuments and changes of street names to celebrate those who had served America and the city.[41] The patriotic intent after the war left the place in a brotherly post-war recovery, which politicians later used to exhibit unity, despite the post-war era also being a time affected by immigration restrictions and surveillance in a continuous search for the ultimate Americanization.[42]

Women's War Experience

The era before the start of the war in 1914 is described as euphoric for women as it was a period of great energy and desire for change,[43] involving everyone from anarchists such as Emma Goldman and Dorothy Day to International Workers of the World leaders such as Elizabeth Gurley Flynn, all of whom knew each other in some way.[44] Women in New York came from all over the country and were often middle-class, but they usually had some form of higher education

---

[40] Ibid., 191-199.
[41] Wilson, *New York and the First World War*, 212-216.
[42] Ibid., 216.
[43] Adickes, *To Be Young Was Very Heaven*, 4-6. For further reading on women's efforts toward emancipation, see Johanna Neumann, *And Yet They Persisted: How American Women Won the Right to Vote* (Hoboken, NJ: John Wiley and Sons, 2020).
[44] Adickes, *To Be Young Was Very Heaven*, 4.

beyond secondary school, which is perhaps how and why this concentrated mass mobilized for and protested against the war in the years to come.[45] Despite the majority of the activists having an education, it was always the case for women in general, thus, some of the leading activists were schooled through political organizations or early trade union experience.[46]

In *The Second Line of Defense*, Lynn Dumenil starts by presenting an incident from 1918 in which a young woman received a poem called "To the Girl I Have Left At Home Behind Me,"[47] in which the imagery is of a soldier whose beloved was sitting at home, quietly and patiently waiting for him as she suffered because of his absence. This portrayal is nowhere near the truth, of which there was an awareness in 1918 when the story was told, because the girl was not sitting at home; she was probably working in a factory, and the soldier knew it. However, the ancient stereotype, according to which his military service was of greater importance and she was just sat prettily waiting for him at home, was not yet about to yield. It was simply not comprehensible that women – from a military point of view – could have actual value in contributing to (and winning) the war.[48]

To claim that there was a large collection of different stances, positions, (work) posts, and opinions from American women toward and during the war is not an overstatement. On the one hand, there were the notable women on the home front keeping society running, making sure that families were taken care of, factories and other commerce were running as usual, etc. On the other hand, there were the pacificists, suffragists, artists, housewives, etc. coming together for one cause or another.

The most interesting thing about this large melting pot is that these groups, all female, had many links because although some worked in factories, they also partook in activism: some did so and were fortunate enough not to need to work, others wished for nothing but peace, while other pacifists had to take radical measures. Thus, as one can imagine, women were connected across all walks of life and political and social stances, joined by the force of their sex and the war.

A group of women who were very obviously praised were those who actually went onto the battlefield, more specifically, the 16,000 American women who

---

[45] Ibid.
[46] Ibid., 5.
[47] Lynn Dumenil, *The Second Line of Defense: American Women and World War I* (Chapel Hill: University of North Carolina Press, 2017), 1.
[48] Ibid.

served in American Expeditionary Forces in France and England, employed directly by the military. Some enlisted for overseas service out of altruism and patriotism, some for the adventure, while others did it for equality with men in the public spheres, as the battlefield was one of the most obvious grounds on which to be equal.[49] Despite American women being segregated into traditionally feminine groups and tasks (e.g. cafeterias, nursing, typing/correspondence, etc.), they were not specifically sheltered from danger, thus, they were literally speaking on equal grounds.

In addition to this new equal ground, this female military mobilization impacted the economy greatly, as it led to women working outside of the home in places that were essential for the modern and bureaucratic way in which this war, unlike previous wars, was led.[50] While American women in the armed forces were limited to specifically female jobs, the (civilian) American women at home gained access, albeit regulated, to male-dominated jobs, such as railroad workers and streetcar conductors; this new shift in dynamics noticeably led to economic change.[51] This shift is exactly what Austin often wrote about in her essays and fought for in her activism on sex emancipation (which she believed the war would help to give a much-needed push forward).

Some scholars do not believe this shift was particularly positive, such as David Kennedy, who writes that, much like other groups, women held excessive hopes for the new way of life for them in the labor market. Women in the Trade Union League spoke of it as it being "the first hour in history for the women of the world... at last, after centuries of disabilities and discrimination, women are coming into the labor and festival of life on equal terms with men."[52] Kennedy deems this joy and statement to be an illusion because, in reality, women's employment in the war was limited and brief, and those who took heavily industrialized jobs to provide for their families had been made to abandon the positions by 1919.[53] Freedom was given to them when it benefitted the political powers, much as it was for African Americans and ethnic groups. It was only about a million women who took war work, and only a few were first-time employees, thus, the 'equal to men' illusion was only that: an illusion.[54] Dumenil discusses how the war created "conventional images of women, especially those that featured their sexual vulnerability ...

---

[49] Venzon, *The United States in the First World War*, 803-804.
[50] Ibid., 803.
[51] Ibid.
[52] Kennedy, *Over Here*, 285.
[53] Ibid.
[54] Ibid.

women as objects to be protected and women themselves as defenders of the nation offered two different messages about the role of men in war."[55] Despite this, women were still oppressed because they were to support the front but also to "remain women and not become freaks."[56] This goes to show the demands which ultimately and clearly wanted women to socially martyr themselves. In *Women and the First World War*, Susan Grayzel writes: "At first, women doctors who offered their services to the military or government directly were rejected."[57] Women were told to contribute, yet when it came to it, they were also told they were not good enough because they were women, even if they were indeed good enough.

Wilson catered to every group in a way that ensured the loyalty he needed at the time, labor women included, because the situation was temporary, and in late 1918, the question of women retiring from the jobs they had held while the men were away was on the horizon again. Women and the black community alike were ensured very little by the war, and it had not fixed the problems at their root. The system was not made to cater to these groups; it simply used them in times of need and wished to return to the natural order once it had no use for them. It might have been a wonderful time for democracy and labor, but it was only on terms that benefitted leaders and ensured no real change or safety from society's racist or oppressive roots. The old order settled slowly back into place, crushing aspirations it had created in the haze of war.[58]

There are two narratives in terms of women and war, one in which women were left behind to maintain the front at home while men were on the battlefield, and another in which women were valid contributors. American women participated in WWI through working in factories, for instance, and taking on traditionally male roles, as well as on the battlefield, even before American troops joined the war in 1917. Wealthy and independent American women, for example, went and joined volunteer units or offered their services independently to the Committees of the French and Belgian Red Cross.[59]

---

[55] Dumenil, *The Second Line of Defense*, 253
[56] Ibid.
[57] Susan R. Grayzel, *Women and the First World War* (New York: Routledge, 2013), 37.
[58] Ibid., 286-288.
[59] Christine E. Hallett, *Veiled Warriors: Allied Nurses of the First World War* (Oxford: Oxford University Press, 2014), 190; Jane Potter, "'I begin to feel as a normal being should, in spite of the blood and anguish in which I move': American Women's First World War Nursing Memoirs," in *First World War Nursing: New Perspectives*, eds. Alison S. Fell and Christine E. Hallett (New York: Routledge, 2013): 51-68.

In New York, parallel with everything else happening, women's suffrage was at its peak along with other movements relating to women.[60] Women were lobbying state by state, which in many ways resembled the American Revolution and the leaderless network moving from state to state to gain momentum.[61] Parallel with the pressures of the war, Wilson also had to face suffragists picketing the White House every day in January of 1917.[62] That February, as 'war fever' gripped the capital, campaigning in wartime was a topic that was on everyone's mind, and President Wilson seemed to use this to get the National American Women's Suffrage Association (NAWSA) on his side by promising to aid them in whatever they needed (according to Carrie Chapman Catt, a promise of which there are no records).[63] What this meeting, and the war situation, resulted in was, for example, Catt abandoning her pacifist beliefs to have the two million members of NAWSA be a resource for the war effort because it was a matter of loyalty for Wilson and Catt.[64] Catt sacrificed her pacifist beliefs for the greater good, and it is worth noting that there were split opinions and stances among the suffrage leaders about America's entrance into the war, some of whom were more against it than others in the business of war criticism and radical pacifism.[65] This makes it clear that among the legacies of WWI, the emancipation of women was among the top outcomes in the USA, and scholars even credit the war as a tipping point because of the pressure of the women's war within the Great War.

New York, being the interesting metropolis it always has been, experienced even greater change politically, both in its governance and in its citizens. New York, as much as it had been the epiphany of the United States, was also a place of unrest precisely because so many groups – ethnic, ideological, and religious – were collected in one place, which made it a suspect place as tensions rose. New York's diversity was scary for the American ideal of an undividable nation, but because of the city's importance to trade and its role

---

[60] Susan Ware, *American Women's History: A Very Short Introduction* (Oxford: Oxford University Press), 78.
[61] For further reading on the concept of leaderless network and revolutionaries, see Clifford Siskin and William Warren, eds., *This Is Enlightenment* (Chicago: University of Chicago Press, 2010).
[62] Neumann, *And Yet They Persisted*, 185.
[63] Ibid., 173.
[64] Ibid., 173-175.
[65] Scott H. Bennett, *Radical Pacifism: The War Resisters League and Gandhian Nonviolence in America, 1915-1963* (Syracuse, NY: Syracuse University Press, 2003), 7-10; Neumann, *And Yet They Persisted*; Ware, *American Women's History*, 80-81.

in the conflict, its place was always highly valued.[66] The examination of New York's urban environment in the context of conflict gives a useful analytical approach to the various (political, social, economic, etc.) changes to the societies, towns, and cities that were at the forefront of the conflict in many different ways, whether militarily, like in Europe, or politically and socially, like in New York. The city was previously an American hotspot but was now the point where politics flourished and from where men and materials were being shipped to the front. The tension and concerns regarding the status of New York and the identity of its citizens continued to worsen with the war's outbreak in 1914, and these became increasingly clear afterward.[67]

Much like the women suffragists' "loyalty for loyalty" idea, the loyalty of the city was of importance. America entered the war to "make the world safe for democracy," and making democracy safe in America was the first step on such a quest; thus, loyalties within the nation itself were essential.[68] People such as Emma Goldman, an anarchist, were a direct challenge to this authoritarian idea, especially in a place like New York, and although there might be a mainstream romanticization of what it was like to be an activist, society proceeded under new laws, such as the Espionage Act, against dissenting opinions, outlawing rebellious views in speeches, the media, etc., while there was also the threat of activists' losing American postage service rights to printed materials/opinions.[69] This goes to show that, just as much as there was propaganda, there was also a lack of freedom of speech in large urban environments such as the Big Apple.

Looking closer to home and perhaps to more shaky ground, the battles on the home front, e.g. female pacifism (and various other forms of activism), were leading the way, even if these were through radical measures, e.g. Carrie Chapman Catt urging women to use any and all measures for peace, even violence, ironically (as these were radicals in terms of not being norm-confirming). The Women's Peace Party was formed in America as early as 1915, forming a new dawn in the American peace movement, as it was dominated and led by women. The inspiration to start such organizations in the United States, even before its entrance into the war, came from the impact

---

[66] Wilson, *New York and the First World War*, 1-18.
[67] Ibid., 38.
[68] Ibid., 158-159. For further reading on American idealism and the thought that they can ensure 'democracy for all,' even to this day, see Kennedy, *Over Here*.
[69] For further reading on the American monitoring of espionage, see Glenn P. Hastedt, *Spies, Wiretaps, and Secret Operations: An Encyclopedia of American Espionage* (Santa Barbara, CA: ABC-Clio, 2011).

of European pacifist feminists,[70] who showcased the horrific scenarios that would ensue if American women did not work to organize themselves for peace.[71] The establishment of these branches all over the world is what later led to international cooperation among notable pacifists, feminists, suffragettes, and so on. The group were critical of the male-dominated peace movement, and the war created the opening needed as the women involved felt a "peculiar moral passion of revolt."[72]

The Women's International League for Peace and Freedom, although it was not officially named until 1919, was a well-oiled machine of an organization that showcases just how women on the home front reacted and mobilized domestically as a reaction to the war.[73] As early as April 1915, women activists and suffragettes from both Europe and the United States gathered at an international conference in The Hague. The meeting's original intent was to discuss matters of international women's suffrage. However, upon the war breaking out less than a year prior to the meeting, the agenda took a drastic turn, and it was matters of war resistance that were at its center.[74] Among the topics were matters of how to oppose the war in Europe, as it was still just a 'European war.'

The women wanted permanent peace, hence the group's early name 'Women for Permanent Peace,'[75] being of the conviction that promoting worldwide social and economic justice, combined with arbitration and mediation, would eventually result in lasting peace worldwide. Much like Austin often reflected on the uniqueness of what the female sex could offer to society at large, this league of women also presented a particular uniqueness in their female efforts for peace.[76] Among the offensives that were set in motion was the encouragement of leaders of neutral countries to negotiate and come to a peaceful solution based on constitutions and suchlike;

---

[70] For example, the speeches of the British feminist pacifist Emmeline Pethick-Lawrence (1867-1954) and the Hungarian Rosika Schwimmer (1877-1948).
[71] Venzon, *The United States in the First World War*, 801.
[72] Ibid.
[73] Ibid, 805-806.
[74] Ibid.
[75] The name used prior to the Women's International League for Peace, which it officially took in 1919.
[76] Venzon, *The United States in the First World War*, 805. For further reading on matters of female efforts toward social reforms, see Helen Rappaport, ed., *Encyclopedia of Women Social Reformers* (Santa Barbara, CA: ABC-Clio, 2001).

however, these encouragements led nowhere, and the conflict continued to escalate until the entry of the United States into the war in 1917.[77]

The female efforts for peace were not always welcome; in fact, in the United States, important suffrage and feminist figures such as Jane Addams (1860-1935)[78] were heavily criticized for their peace efforts, forcing American activists to want just a peace settlement because the large collaboration between women from so many nations was perhaps uncanny and reason to be accused of treason in such a rigid global conflict situation.[79] However, it is worth noting that the peace effort was not new; Addams, for example, had been among the founders of the Anti-Imperialist League branch in Chicago as far back as 1899, because even then there had been reason to be critical, and part of Addams' perceptive was that empire was bringing out the most violent, destructive aspects of American society, resulting in the brutalization of American culture, thereby linking her peace activism with her suffragism like many other women in her circle.[80] The belief that Addams and like-minded women in America held was that the lives of countless people intertwined to the point where nationalism had to make way for internationalism and patriotism for humanitarianism, which, needless to say, went against the norm.[81] Thus, the peace efforts demonstrated by many had deep roots, and those were growing ever deeper due to the war.

It was women such as this who inspired Austin, who even cites Jane Addams in the bibliography of her works, e.g *The Young Woman Citizen* references Addams' work on democracy and social ethics in matters concerning Americanization.[82]

Austin's War Experience

> I am heartily agreed that war – the knockdown and drag method – is stupid, wasteful and often unsatisfactory. But it remains a method which many powerful people insist on using.[83]
>
> Mary Hunter Austin (1917)

---

[77] Ibid.
[78] Robin Kadison Berson, *Jane Addams: A Biography* (Westport, CT: Greenwood Press, 2004), 52. Adams was also the organizer of the Woman's Peace Party in 1915.
[79] Verzon, *The United States in the First World War*, 805.
[80] Richard Seymour, *American Insurgents: A Brief History of American Anti-Imperialism* (Chicago: Haymarket Books, 2012), 52.
[81] Ibid.
[82] Jane Addams, *Democracy and Social Ethics* (New York: Macmillan, 1902).
[83] Mary Hunter Austin, "Women as Pacifists," *New York Tribune*, February 17, 1917, 8.

The strongest correlation we can see in Austin's writing and person, as well as in society as a whole, with the war is that work was the key to freedom. Work would lead to independence and, cyclically, independence would lead to the breaking of gender norms and stereotypes as well as financial security, because the latter would lead the world to a more balanced non-violent state. New York City was a haven for social and political rebels, revolutionaries, and radicals such as Austin. Greenwich Village was described as the middle ground of orchestrated American Revolution attempts and so forth.[84] The outbreak of the war in Europe created a new order in society after 1914, and residents across communities were asked to demonstrate their allegiance to the United States, a process which only intensified as the nation became involved in the conflict in 1917.[85]

Mary Austin, "one of the most distinguished women of letters in America, advocates economic independence for all girls as a safeguard for their self-respect and a justification for their existence in a working world."[86] This is evidence of how the war impacted her views and work toward sex emancipation and, in a stereotype of the time, toward avoiding the "old maid's fate," which suggests that without a man one is not worth much, let alone being in possession of any real self-respect; thus, the war became the largest aid in trying to battle this fate of so many. The universal mobilization of women, according to Austin's like-minded peers, would contribute to America's preparedness and look after the best interests of its riches.[87] It was clear that America and the world's eyes were starting to see the values of women because, as newspapers printed in discussions on the new meaning of the term 'mobilization' during the critical years of American interference, "the world mobilize is generally used about soldiers ... or rather, I should say that it was generally used about soldiers before the European war. But since 1914 the world has learned many things."[88] The people were mobilizing more for the humanitarian activities of the First World War than any war before, and volunteers of all genders helped with battlefield needs as well as held the fort in the new structures of society.[89]

---

[84] Wilson, *New York and the First World War*, 14-15.
[85] Ibid., 21.
[86] Marguerite Mooers Marshall, "Mobilizing the American Girl into an Industrial Reserve Force Is Insurance Against Oldmaid's Fate," *The Evening World*, March 6, 1917, 3.
[87] Ibid.
[88] "Uncle Harry Tells about Mobilizing the Nation's Industries," *Evening Journal*, 17.
[89] "Mobilization of Civil Activities in Preparing War Hospital Equipment," *The Sunday Star*, March 25, 1917, 12.

Austin was quick to be a good example of an active woman, and in addition to activism and food supply relief, she also contributed to the *Belgian Relief Cook Book* along with other famous men and women, written in order to aid Belgium in the war.[90] This is not surprising, as many of the newspaper mentions of the writer in regards to her activism were often accompanied by other famous New York women of significance. For instance, she was described in a list of writers *The Sun* claimed to be brilliant, a newspaper that was strongly popular with the working class.[91] Later on, in 1916, as tensions continued to rise in Europe and America's role was further disputed at home, Austin was named among a list of 'Notable Writers' who were discussing the demand for optimism.[92] The writer's message was about how she believed that literature is shaped by evasive idealism instead of realism, highlighting the start of the war.[93]

In addition to commenting on literary aspects in war times, the author and activist was also one of the main voices in opening the debate about how to solve the problem of the overflow of women in Europe as a result of the war.[94] However, she believed that "[t]he change the war has brought about has been to give untold numbers of women interesting and worth-while labor.... Willy-nilly they have had to turn aside from being wives and mothers to be tramcar conductors and postmen."[95] This ideology later became the fundamental idea of how she believed American women should make themselves a resource during the war. If anything is direct evidence of the changed gender roles during the war, it is this. Austin strove to be among the women who made a change for change's sake and for the upkeep of morality when she selflessly attempted to mobilize women. Austin not only spoke about these things but actively made efforts to contribute to change, for example, as president of the Child Welfare League, where she sat alongside women from other organizations in a committee to prepare females efficiently for war.[96]

What the war contributed to Mary Hunter Austin is that it proved her fundamental beliefs of female strength correct, because as far back as 1911, Austin was quoted in newspapers as saying, "I think that is most important

---

[90] "Belgian Relief Cook Book," *New York Tribune*, December 12, 1915, 4.
[91] "Is the British Novel Superior to the American Novel?" *The Sun*, April 18, 1916, 7.
[92] "Notable Writers Discuss the Demand For Optimism," *The Sun*, April 15, 1916, 10.
[93] Ibid.
[94] "War Problem of Superfluous Woman May Be Solved by Industry or Polygamy: Old Maiden of Past Ages Will Disappear," *The Evening World*, July 25, 1916, 3
[95] "The Superfluous Women," *New York Tribune*, July 30, 1916, 20.
[96] "National Council Plans Woman's Part in War," *The Evening Star*, April 4, 1917, 9.

that every woman should be able to take care of herself by her own labor. And she should not only be able – she should do it. This applies to the married woman just as much as to the unmarried ones. It is of course not necessary or advisable that every woman should work outside the home, but she should be economically independent whether she is working for her husband in his house or someone else in an office."[97] These ideas for independence got an opportunity to flourish during mobilization. Austin's correlation with the war was an impactful one, and it clearly shows that her fundamental beliefs developed greatly as a result. Although she was active in American suffrage meetings and other political events, in the early years of the war, it is said that her mind was only occupied by "the European war" for a brief moment, relating only to concerns about food conservation.[98] This is not to say that the author was self-absorbed, but it does show how lightly most Americans, even politically active individuals such as Austin, thought about the war as it probably did not feel like an American problem but a European one, which she wanted to help to solve.

As mentioned, Austin's concerns were not ones relating to the military and destruction, as perhaps nobody could foresee the war resulting in the deaths of 6,000 people a day for 1,500 days,[99] but were rather about aiding with food supplies, which is closely related to the gender roles of the time.[100] Austin's war effort in New York, thus, became related to conserving leftover food, which was to be shipped over to help the Europeans. Austin, although inspired by New York, often longed to leave it,[101] which is perhaps much of the reason why she did not entirely mobilize herself in a fully militant manner like other women critical of the war to begin with. An extraordinary moment for her during the war was her attendance at a suffrage meeting in Atlantic City, where President Wilson spoke to a militant assemblage of women who were determined on matters of voting rights in 1916.[102] Austin was electrified by President Wilson's drive and words, and upon the Americans' entrance into

---

[97] "Mrs. Well Known Says," *The Times,* January 9, 1911, 2.
[98] Fink, *I-Mary,* 172.
[99] Merriman, *Modern Europe,* 1082.
[100] For further reading on Mary Hunter Austin's impact on gender roles, see Jowan A. Mohammed, "Mary Hunter Austin und die Forderungen nach einer Veränderung der Geschlechterrollen in den USA, 1914-1918," in *Geschlecht und Klassenkampf: Die „Frauenfrage" aus deutscher und internationaler Perspektive im 19. und 20. Jahrhundert,* eds. Vincent Streichhahn and Frank Jacob (Berlin: Metropol Verlag, 2020), 222-239.
[101] Fink, *I-Mary,* 176.
[102] Mary Austin to Ina Cassidy, October 14, 1916, Cassidy Family Papers, The Bancroft Library, University of California, Berkeley, Box 7, cited in Fink, *I-Mary,* 280.

the war, it was clear that her motivation had increased, as she believed that such fighting as a means of "getting something done"[103] was a valedictory to her life as a feminist.[104]

In a short newspaper article titled "Women as Pacifists" in the *New York Tribune*, one of the nation's leading Republican daily news, published in February 1917, two months before the US joined the war, Austin wrote about why she felt "Constrained to Resign from the Women's Peace Party" and why she believed in the existence of a struggle of "Feminism vs. Society as a Whole," which showcased her diversity.[105] Previously, one could argue about the rebelliousness in her ideology to place the interests of women ahead of society as a whole; thus, she did not speak radically alone but as part of a movement. Feminists were more rebellious than traditional suffragettes and socialists, who were deemed truer to the concept of female virtue despite their fights.[106] Austin maintained that women were against war because it threatened their subjective interests more than the interests of any other class in society. Since the war was claiming the lives of men, it ensured men's place in society and the privileges of men only. Women's fear of bloody battles was not irrational, as war deprived them of their opportunity to claim a place in society when men went to fight these battles, leaving women groundless. One can gather why the number of female pacifists was proportionally higher, because war demanded more of women than it gave them in return.[107] However, the subject comes more to light in Austin's distaste for war, because she developed the idea that female pacifists, particularly the strong peace movement, were equally as selfish as those who wished for war, because the two sides (war or peace) demanded the same amount of selfishness. This idea that the peace movement was just agenda-based was something that the capital later pushed as it followed up on American involvement in the war.[108] The intention to shed light on women's productivity appeared to continue with newspaper headlines such as the notable "Mobilizing the American Girl into an Industrial Reserve Force Is

---

[103] Mary Austin to H. G. Wells, January 24, 1917, Mary Hunter Austin Collection, The Huntington Library, San Marino, CA, cited in Goodman and Dawson, *Mary Austin and the American West*, 295.

[104] Mary Austin to Houghton Mifflin, January 8, 1918, Cassidy Family Papers, Box 6, cited in Fink, *I-Mary*, 281.

[105] Mary Hunter Austin, "Women as Pacifists," *New York Tribune*, February 17, 1917, 8.

[106] Adickes, *To Be Young Was Very Heaven*, 89.

[107] Mary Hunter Austin, "Women as Pacifists," *New York Tribune*, February 17, 1917, 8.

[108] "Women and War," *The Washington Times* (Washington, DC), February 1917, 6.

Insurance Against Old Maid's Fate."[109] The article's intent was to encourage and shed light on contributing to women's independence through them earning their own living, pointing to Mary Austin as one of the most prominent female advocates for women's economic independence.[110]

Despite Austin's notable writing activities in New York City, her literary obtainability suffered because of the war.[111] *The Young Woman Citizen* was promoted as a "penetrating analysis of the obligations of citizenship which are assumed by men and women with the wish to vote"[112] and was reviewed as "a book that masculine as well as feminine voters will find well worth studying."[113] The book is a discussion of the problems of democracy and of the responsibility that Americans bear toward building world democracy, to which she believed the United States was wholeheartedly committed. The author insists that there must be "conscious preparation for citizenship as wide as the world itself."[114] Wilson confirmed that despite the lack of American involvement in the early years of the war, its authority was still ever-present where matters of identity and citizenship were concerned.[115] This explains Austin's alarmed debates on the subject matter of the citizenship of women in her writing and activism. *The Young Woman Citizen* is often described as attention-grabbing and as having democracy at its heart, for example, as "[a]n incisive re-interpretation of the responsibilities of citizenship in its relation to universal democracy that commands the attention of thinking people."[116] Austin herself previously claimed that *The Young Woman Citizen* was the one that was closest to her heart and that its financial failure was in many ways devastating for her. The war directly affected the author's financial situation, as her works got held up before manufacturing, as did their increase in price, meaning fewer sales as times were tight.[117]

---

[109] Marguerite Mooers Marshall, "Mobilizing the American Girl into an Industrial Reserve Force Is Insurance Against Oldmaid's Fate," *The Evening World*, March 6, 1917, 3.
[110] Ibid.
[111] "Book News," *New York Tribune*, February 2, 1918, 7.
[112] "The Young Woman Citizen," *The Sun*, June 16, 1918, 15.
[113] Dorothy Scarborough, "Mary Austin to 'The Young Woman Citizen,'" *The Sun*, December 29, 1918, 9.
[114] Ibid.
[115] Wilson, *New York and the First World War*, 15.
[116] "The Young Woman Citizen," *New York Tribune*, November 9, 1918, 9.
[117] "Books and the Book World" *The Sun*, October 13, 1918, 6.

This quest for preparedness continued for Austin as well as other famous writers in the name of mobilization and preparedness.[118] She also continued with her own ideologies in the years to come, as she encouraged women to take on jobs as far and wide as possible. The enthusiastic author was depicted as firmly believing that women brought special capabilities to politics. These capabilities included attributes that their previous occupations and feminine insight strengthened. Women's instinct for a new social direction, and their habits of thinking the next thing, enabled them to keep ideas in a state of continuous mobilization and development. The idea was promoted that this capacity of intuitive judgment was the contribution that women had to bring to their new undertaking. The validation of what women could bring to the table, unlike men, is in understanding what was valued, rather than what they would do as men could.[119] The author's message is clear in that women would take jobs and demand space, but they would "only take jobs that rightfully belong to them," although Austin also claimed that more change was needed since only the existence of a "woman voter will make democracy real," as another Marguerite Mooers Marshall newspaper article from 1918 reported.[120]

Mary Hunter Austin understood that Americans needed to be presented with realism instead of just evasive optimism, and her years in New York made her advocate this.[121] The author supported other women and their causes, writing that "I did not care so much where the women were going who went after war honors... women walking on their hind legs. We saw a great deal of them, and gave them what they wanted."[122]

Austin was among a bulk of female writers who wished to contribute to the trying times by dedicating their writing to help the patriotic drive and promote problem-solving in wartime,[123] and thus how her ideas impacted society and how society impacted her writing in this period can clearly be seen in her works and her activism.

---

[118] "Authors and Artists are Mobilizing for Preparedness," *The Sun*, March 25, 1917, 2.
[119] Dorothy Scarborough, "Mary Austin to 'The Young Woman Citizen,'" *The Sun*, December 29, 1918, 9.
[120] Marguerite Mooers Marshall, "Women's New Citizenship Means Men in Men's Job Prophecy of Mary Austin," *The Evening World*, May 15, 1918, 16.
[121] "Patriotic Women Authors Will Write for America," *The Sun*, May 5, 1917, 6.
[122] Austin, *Earth Horizon*, 328.
[123] "Patriotic Women Authors Will Write for America," *The Sun*, May 5, 1917, 6.

Chapter 3

Mary Hunter Austin's Writings (1917-1920)

This chapter will be a literature review chapter that takes an analytical look at the primary works of Mary Hunter Austin between 1917 and 1920 in order to highlight overlooked works that were not necessarily intended as feminist, in addition to some very directly feminist essays and works – the variation will give an insight into her diversity both as a writer and as a woman in her own time as well as her legacy beyond it. The close readings are supposed to link the texts to their respective historical contexts and personal motives to provide more than solely a literary analysis, which does not serve the purpose of this book, i.e. the identification of the author's attitude toward the war and the latter's impact on Austin's thoughts. The works include *The Ford* (1917), *The Young Woman Citizen* (1918), and *No. 26 Jayne Street* (1920), as well as the 1918 article "Sex Emancipation Through War," which are all of particular interest because of the strong impact of the First World War in those years and the social and political changes of the time. The works discuss relevant social and political questions in fictional settings, with the exceptions of *The Young Woman Citizen* and "Sex Emancipation," which are direct sociological/political analyses of and constructive contributions to the society and politics of the time. Austin wrote both fiction that was more social and domestic (e.g. *The Ford*) and more directly political pieces (e.g. "Sex Emancipation" and *The Young Woman Citizen*). The reason to boil down Austin's many works, which include hundreds of articles and tens of books, into only a few is that these works run in parallel with the war, which is the essence of the examination in this research.

These four main literary works are significant because Austin leaves her Native American writing tradition and ventures into themes more related to gender and socialism, which can be linked to the global situation of the time. In order to supplement the analysis, this chapter will also look at more celebrated works by Austin, such as *A Woman of Genius* (1912), which is more autobiographical fiction that can be found in the anthology *American Voices: American Women* (1973) by Lee R. Edwards and Arlyn Diamond, as well as her own autobiography *Earth Horizon*, which has been used throughout this book. The supplement *Earth Horizon* provides more than anything is how Austin wished to be seen, perhaps differently from how she actually was.

The literature in question has, in later years, been marked as books of significant value for their contribution to philosophical, classical, scientific, religious, historical, and mythological questions. Thus, the present analysis will take a closer look at Austin's relationship with the historical events of the First World War and, at the same time, try to evaluate the war's impact on the American writer. This chapter will provide summaries of the works and see how Austin interpreted the war as it related to the gender roles of the time. How far the experience of the First World War changed Austin's views on gender norms and roles, as they existed in the United States during the first years of the 20th century, also has to be considered. The extent to which Austin criticized the existence of such norms will also be analyzed. Did she do it as a socialist or as an activist for women's rights? The author was described as an "almost pure intellect," indicating that she was in fact not a contributing factor to a so-called "sentimentalization of women" and that she was forgiven because her books are neither cynical nor too long.[1] She is labeled as someone of great value in this debate on the strength of female writers and is often connected to figures such as Elizabeth Jordan (1865-1947), Inez Gilmore (1873-1970), Amélie Rives (1863-1945), and many other important female writers of worth at the time.

The Ford (1917)

Summary

The Brent family are the main protagonists of the book, and the events of the plot revolve around their deteriorating economy as ranch owners. The unfortunate economic situation is due to an intense drought in the valley, which makes the land impossible to work on and profit from. The story focuses on land moguls (who are oil prospectors) who come to the valley and attempt to scheme landowners out of the natural resources in the land by buying it on the cheap, since they are experiencing hard times. The intentions of these moguls are to 'rob' the valley of its water and oil in a bigger business and consumer plot, thus making regional development in a rural native landscape one of the book's central storylines. This story of water wars is based on real events that occurred to Austin and her family, however *The Ford*'s political undertone draws on other narratives as well. Ironically, the family's aim is to seek opportunities for oil in the city, along with other families who sell their land in their old area. Seeking the same oil they were 'robbed' of in the first place is what leads to the destruction of the land, because the fields are no longer agriculturally viable. From an analytical perspective, this can be read as capitalist criticism; it is also indubitable that

---

[1] Gertrude Atherton "The Authors Arbitrate," *The Sun*, May 2, 1914, 9

the war did not impact the author's writing as it was unfolding at the same time as she was writing it, despite the plot being inspired by previous events.

The plot focuses on Kenneth Brent and his sister Anne, who portray innocence, as opposed to the scheming buyers. The novel's highest hierarchical landlord is "Old Man" Rickart, who eventually monopolizes the land, taking it away from its former owners, and takes control of the construction of a pipeline. Anne becomes determined to buy back her family's land when she grows up and therefore becomes a successful real estate agent in her adulthood (as well as being educated in/familiar with land laws). Her brother Kenneth does not have the same vision of fighting the capitalist system in order to get back their family land, but instead grows up to become a lawyer and, ironically, a clerk for Rickart. The old Rickart is both a symbolic and literary character, making him the embodiment of capitalism. Rickart represents the complete opposite of what the protagonists stand for; artful in business at the cost of others, he is everything Austin's activism and ideologies were against.

The plot goes into the character growth and development of Kenneth and Anne and comes full circle when they end up back where they started: fighting the man. Kenneth's meeting with his childhood friend Virginia, who is now a suffragette-like figure who goes to rallies and demonstrates against big corporations, inspires him to take a look at himself. Anne and Kenneth plot together to bring knowledge to the people about what is happening to the land through using their legal knowledge and skills to bring down the man. The story ends more positively than the real water war events that took place in Austin's own life, which actually became a major cause of instability to her finances and marriage.

Analysis

As previously mentioned, *The Ford* draws from Austin's personal experience of when she and her husband went through the Owens Valley water crisis in the early 1900s. However, the setting of the plot has been altered to the fictional Tierra Longa Valley and San Francisco instead of the Owens Valley and Los Angeles. The setting contains both urban and rural spaces, creating parallels in both nature as well as the government, which come through with the corporate power that Austin often criticized from a socialist and pacifist perspective. The reason this book is chosen here, although it is fiction and its plot is far away from the war-related themes of other works presented in this book, is that the Mary Hunter Austin of 1917 who wrote it was obviously affected by the climate around her. The author's ideologies at the time of writing the story are clearly impacted by a much more evolved characteristic as an impact of social and political change.

When reading this analysis, one might think that it is perhaps a stretch to claim any correlation between the war and Austin; however, considering the fact that the United States entered the war in April of 1917, while *The Ford* was published in October, and taking into account the suspense long prior to April, it is not a stretch to stand by the notion that the war definitely impacted the intellectual and political ideas and self-awareness that many of the characters in the book possess as the book and the war were parallel events. Austin's consciousness was without any argument affected by the war as she was an activist who was engaged not only in political matters long before America's actual interference in the war but in all matters of society – not just war-related ones. The author was exposed to grander ideas than she had been when going through the events of the water crisis in her own experience, which impacted her ideas/perspectives on things, thus impacting her narratives in a sense. Her marriage, no matter how dull, was positively impacted by the events that inspired *The Ford*; thus, in parts, it is believed that Stafford standing up and taking part in the action was among the events that excited her.

Austin, much like other intellectuals, was only as great as her continuous personal development and growth, which of course the war affected; thus, the conclusion that this book is not significantly influenced by the political landscape of the time is unavoidable. Perhaps if the book had been written a decade prior to the war, the way in which Austin wrote the symbolism in each character and plotline would not be so greatly correlated to those relevant to themes of power balance, equality, social status, etc. In this book, the author's landscape writer background is still very present, as the descriptions of nature are significant in the story and give the reader an insight into how the author feels about the unjust measures taken for the domestication of the land and that justice might eventually be served "as though they plotted to tear loose at any moment and stamp out the little hordes of men." However, it is a representation of power dynamics, which are parallel to any political issues (the war was ongoing at the time of the book's publication). Furthermore, the use of the landscape as a literary effect proves Austin's early eco-activism for wildlife, which was often evident in her writing about Native Americans.

John Peterson discusses the "Transregional Networks in Mary Austin's *The Ford*"[2] and has similar ideas to Norwood and Blend, one of which concerns Anne's ability to negotiate the transregional forces that threaten the valley from a gender perspective; this is female empowerment. From a climate/

---

[2] John Peterson, "The Interconnected Bioregion: Transregional Networks in Mary Austin's *The Ford*," *Western American Literature: A Journal of Literary, Cultural, and Place Studies* 52, no. 1 (2017): 160.

sustainability perspective, Peterson's research attempts to portray that Austin was in many ways sixty years ahead of her time by narrating such a plot when the bioregional movement (the advocacy that human prints should mainly be constrained by ecological or geographical boundaries rather than political ones) was not yet in existence (it would not be founded until the 1970s).[3] From a gender perspective, this can be read as a truly powerful pledge for Anne's character as a woman, as well as Austin's perception at the time. Nature as a gender-empowerment factor can also be detected in *Women and Nature: Saving the "Wild" West* by Glenda Riley. Riley credits Austin as challenging gender norms because of her descriptions of the white man as materialistic and exploitative and her white women as understanding and sympathetic to the land. Austin's landscape's relation to gender is pinpointed as an opportunity for women to "walk off" the societal values which bound them at the time.[4]

Nature is crucial in the story because the novelist takes ownership of the wilderness through her writing and uses it as a tool to show the landscape as something that surpasses and resists masculine dominance.[5] This is a fact that can be linked to and at the same time emphasizes the injustice women felt in their fight for equality. In the battle, Anne is assigned a role in the resisting army, which ultimately is a gendered power move because it is men that she is directing. One can recognize many of these actions as battles of domination and inequality, among which are the racial divides of the people in the story (the Native Americans vs. the whites).[6] The focus on nature, in addition to the idea of 'the wild woman' trope, is also one that can clearly be linked to religion. The author's Christian roots are evident in this book through symbolism.[7] The first section of the book, dealing with the coming of age, heavily relies on the biblical narrative, e.g. in the games they play as children – and the correlation between Jacob wrestling with God and Kenneth's journey into maturity.[8]

The suffragist, socialist, and poet Dora Montefiore (1851-1933) wrote in 1909 that "It has often been said that the twentieth century will be the century of

---

[3] Ibid.
[4] Glenda Riley, *Women and Nature: Saving the "Wild" West* (Lincoln, NE: University of Nebraska Press, 1999), 63.
[5] Blend, "Mary Austin and the Western Conservation Movement," 25.
[6] Peterson, "The Interconnected Bioregion," 171.
[7] For a further analysis of the religious roots in *The Ford*, see Peterson, "Wrestling with 'Half Gods'."
[8] Ibid., 657.

women; and this means, of course, to us Social-Democratic women, that women, as well as men, will be called upon to play a conscious part in the struggle that will only come to an end when the world has been gained for the workers."[9] Portraying the mainstream understanding, however, in "For White Men Only: The Socialist Party of America and Issues of Gender, Ethnicity and Race," Professor Sally M. Miller examines the experience of the distinct groups within the Socialist Party of America.[10]

Miller's take is that despite the advocacy of inclusion, with an initiation offered to members irrespective of gender or color, the implementation was perhaps lacking; although it explains Austin's (and so many others') attraction to the party's principles and ideologies, in practice it was less inclusive.[11] However, the understanding, particularly at the time of the publication of *The Ford*, was that inclusion without gender or race bias was something that people longed for. Similar to the situation with regard to women, despite the welcome, the relationship between the Socialist Party in America and immigrants was never strongly established and lacked a firm foundation, leaving the immigrant workers without much support.[12] What was promised did not match what was practiced.

Susan Goodman and Carl Dawson discuss, in their 2009 publication *Mary Austin and the American West*, that this is to be connected to Austin questioning the fundamental rights of anyone taking over land that was not theirs but had instead been granted to them by the Spanish Crown during colonization.[13] It is a direct criticism of society and its political institutions, which is essentially what the main takeaway of this book should be. The story is about the struggle between city and valley and wrongful claims to resources.[14] Consider also that WWI turned New York into a site of resource struggle; as the United States mobilized for war entrance, the city was used as a place to ship out men and materials.[15]

---

[9] Dora B. Montefiore, *The Position of Women in the Socialist Movement* (London: Twentieth Century Press, 1909).
[10] Miller, "For White Men Only," 283.
[11] Ibid.
[12] Ibid., 290.
[13] Goodman and Dawson, *Mary Austin and the American West*, 55.
[14] Hoffman, "Mary Austin," 307.
[15] For further reading about New York as a resource haven and the problems the war brought, see Maffi, *Gateway to the Promised Land*; Wilson, *New York and the First World War*.

"The greatest common factor of the Tierra Longans was their general inability to rise to the Old Man's measure; they were inferior stuff of the same pattern,"[16] Austin echoes in *The Ford*, in direct disagreement with Herbert Hoover, whose politics she had been in disagreement with since the beginning of the war.[17] Austin and Hoover were in close agreement, according to Goodman and Dawson, in terms of volunteer work to provide Europe with food supplies (the Food Relief Campaign), however disagreements emerged when Austin demanded that Hoover should broaden his efforts from food to matters of women and child labor; these demands were not met.[18] Austin wished to change the roots of the family structure with the intention of improving matters of food and work, but Hoover was content with the efforts being made through the Food Relief Campaign. This narrative of changing society from its roots, i.e. family structures, is a red line that can be traced through all of the works. Again, this goes to show that, when it came to questions of domestic gender structures, the author's intentions were to make positive and permanent changes to politics.

The writer drives the narrative of the collapse of cultural value, and potentially civilization, which is portrayed in all three of her literary works that are discussed here; she believed and tried to portray through this novel that any system that rested on ignorance and "that strange, ineradicable quality of men called righteousness"[19] was doomed in many ways. In the story, Kenneth reaches a point of growth when he put his male-driven righteousness aside and finally takes the time to listen to his sister, Anne, and comes to the realization that they have read the same books yet come to widely different conclusions.[20] This is a point where a male character opens his eyes to the potential of a woman in a way that Austin herself so often advocated in real life, for instance by speaking about making women more resourceful for society. Here, gender is both critiqued as well as constructively challenged, as Austin portrays a transformation that breaks gender barriers. The author's criticism of gender roles comes through and is a theme that is often approached, both in her literature and her real-life actions.

Anne's strong character replies to this surprise that "Women have a much keener sense of real values." She speaks in reference to their different points of view, for instance on the topic of marriage. The claim is that a woman will

---

[16] Austin, *The Ford*, 403.
[17] Goodman and Dawson, *Mary Austin and the American West*, 162.
[18] Ibid., 158.
[19] Ibid., 161.
[20] Austin, *The Ford*, 233.

marry a man because he is tidy and truthful, which will make him a good father, but a man will not marry a woman unless she makes him feel a particular way. The main idea to take away from such a claim is that gender roles are constructed in many ways because women think practically and with a long-term view, while men are self-serving and get rewarded for it simply because of their sex. This is a direct criticism of gender and social norms, because essentially what Austin believed was that "Love in man may change his relation to society, but in woman it changes the woman."

This is particularly seen in the case of Anne Brent, who not only grows up to be a smart, independent, and hardworking woman, but also continues to show determination throughout the storyline until its peak and triumph when she stands up to the Old Man. Here, the Old Man can resemble a patriarchal society that women have to stand up against, or he can be interpreted as the embodiment of capitalism (which is evil and needs standing up to in the story). One notable incident occurs early on while the main protagonists are still young when Anne reveals her wish to buy back her family's land.[21] When she tells the younger Kenneth about this plan, her statement is met with disbelief because she only has seven hundred dollars at the time, and thus her brother says it is "the sort of thing a girl might do."[22] This was partly due to being hurt by his exclusion from the plans, about which Anne is so confident.[23] Thus, it is no surprise that Austin gives her the strength and value to push the plot of the story more than it pushes her.

This strong female drive is heavily inspired by the suffragette movement of the time in New York in particular and in the United States in general. *The Ford* is about land, funds and resources, protests, and females coming together to organize themselves and be of value alongside men. Anne seemed determined from a young age that she did not want to get married and as such is portrayed as a firm believer that girls do not have to get married.[24] This core belief is defended by other characters, who describe "women like her" as being more about the property right to their womanhood than anything else.[25] This reflects American society in 1917, as women were doing just that in terms of validation for themselves at the critical time of war developments in the United States. They were joining unions and mobilizing themselves just

---

[21] Ibid., 167.
[22] Ibid., 168.
[23] Ibid., 269.
[24] Ibid., 170.
[25] Ibid., 209.

as much as men, particularly because of the global situation; however, as it was based on their gender, it was a permanent state of mobilization.[26]

Kenneth, on the other hand, seems to be in disbelief that it is not preposterous for him, as a man, to go to San Francisco and *demand* to be taught the art of "getting things from people," as he had observed in the devious Mr. Rickart, and in his quest to get there he had studied law to be of great use to Rickart (who symbolizes capitalism, which is very much accepted, unlike the female characters of the story).[27] Much to Kenneth's disappointment, the reality was ugly, as the Old Man only hired men to tell them how to work around laws in his own favor, no matter who he stepped on. This is exactly the sort of thing the radical socialists of New York prided themselves on fighting, particularly at a time when the government discouraged strikes, but the matter was ever-present in the form of issues with labor welfare and propaganda marking the dissatisfaction of workers with disloyalty.[28] This important social issue of propaganda and labor trouble is portrayed in the story through the character of Virginia, who, despite an upper-class background, is a greater truth beyond her sheltered and privileged upbringing.[29] She goes on to explain that because of her status, she ought to marry a man of status, who would naturally be too busy for her, thus leaving her unsatisfied. Virginia is said to be the organizer of laborers later on, and it is labor trouble that brings her back into Kenneth and Anne's lives (parallel with the development of the struggles with unionism).[30] Virginia shows up because she is an organizer, and Kenneth, in a moment of recollecting their childhood, says that "I've no doubt she's good at it. Virginia could always make people play her game."[31] Among the rallies that Virginia is said to organize is one for a women's trade union, and she later inspires Kenneth to finally stand up to the capitalistic, soulless old man that he works for as a lawyer. Virginia's labor activism becomes Kenneth's new drive to work for justice. This is particularly important in the story as well as for modern interpretations because it shows a narrative where women inspire positive change within society and in the opposite sex. Kenneth is unable to follow the Old Man's example, as he had originally intended, and the appropriate new direction becomes following Virginia, which ultimately is also the most ethical

---

[26] Gabrielson, "Woman-Thought," 656.
[27] Austin, *The Ford*, 168-176.
[28] Kennedy, *Over Here*, 71.
[29] Ibid., 180.
[30] Ibid., 179.
[31] Ibid.

path in the story. Kenneth comes to terms with the fact that he is done with big business: "if I'm done with Rickart, it's because I'm done with his way of doing business."[32] This principle was widespread within the Socialist Party at a time when, according to historians, this radicalism was in the air.[33] It was a common trait in society to go on strike to demonstrate against the old ways of businesses, and the practice was widespread in America.[34]

The plot finally reaches the point of the Old Man's failure to gain control over Tierra Longa's resources, and the reader can finally feel a wholesome triumph when victory is reached through successful negotiations. Naturally, this is a victory led by a male hero, assisted by female characters, though in many ways it shows strength from both, even though men are the ones on the battlefield, figuratively speaking. This can, in fact, be especially linked to the war, as Austin claimed this connection several times throughout the course of American interference in the First World War, because her pacifistic belief was that men never lost their identity in war, even though women are the biggest losers because they are invalidated without a male companion.

Despite the plot being heavy and descriptive, *The Ford* is a story that values female resources and self-awareness: Austin believed that by saying that if a woman is denied her rights and if someone is to stand in her way, then she should be allowed to cut and run and be understood for the decision.[35] This is a particular reference to Austin's own 'flexible' pacifism, as she often preached that women should not be afraid of bloody battles if that is what it took to obtain justice. This example also strengthens the link between the women's movement toward 1920 and the Nineteenth Amendment.[36] In *The Ford*, Austin is in many ways still true to her identity as a nature writer, inspired by real events that took place in her own life – this analysis is less about *The Ford* itself and more about Austin. The book's political motives make this a story about disagreeing with the Old Man, which can be linked to Austin's disapproval of the United States joining the First World War for imperialist and capitalist reasons. In regard to the critical narrative/approach to capitalism, the socialist perspective is the main impactful component/inspiration.

The author takes the opportunity in this novel to criticize the overgrowth of big business and capitalism as a reason for the war, which is a narrative that continues throughout her later writings during the war years. With the

---

[32] Austin, *The Ford*, 406.
[33] Adickes, *To Be Young Was Very Heaven*, 9-20.
[34] Ibid.
[35] Ibid.
[36] Mary Hunter Austin, "Women as Pacifists," *New York Tribune*, February 17, 1917, 8.

development of the anti-war movement, the uprising of the suffragettes against society, as well as the growth of a broader understanding of injustices in terms of gender, women were not equal and, in areas where they were welcomed with the promise of inclusion, they often experienced some level of segregation, for example within political parties. Suffragettes were content with their maternal role, which Austin was in many ways against.[37] Austin's characters, despite being fictional, were all based on ideas, because they had become her beliefs and were the embodiments of philosophies and ideologies, e.g. Kenneth resembling capitalism, which Austin was against. New York further developed her skills and her as a person because it was the center for political as well as intellectual development, which is why her socialist ideas grew more there than at any other time. She believed that settling for less was not enough, which is what club women did when they continued to conserve their 'womanhood' as their main trait.[38] The quest to seek new gender roles seemed like a more permanent solution, instead of going back to the old ways simply because of biology.

Just as her fictional characters partake in demonstrations, the author also got involved in such activities herself, which is why it can be concluded that this book is more a manifesto of everything she wanted to be the epiphany of: a critical voice to lead the way. For example, Austin is said to have participated in suffrage activities that were reported on a daily basis.[39] Her name was associated with meetings related to "chairmen of all congressional union processions," in which Austin's position was "chairman of arrangements for the procession."[40] *The Evening Star* reports on the author attending parades in Washington to speak to leaders and build bridges.[41] She is said to have been "rich in color and dramatic in effect,"[42] which highlights the essence of her exoticism as a person. Drama as a method was something often associated with the writer and activist, and the title of the article "Mary Austin, Author and Dramatist, Here To Aid In Great Suffrage Parade, Is Constructive Pacifists, and Claims That Peace Will Come Only After It Has Been Made Dramatic"[43] is more or less typical of all the articles about the suffrage parade's intention to steer toward dramatic effects. To give another example, *The Washington Times*

---

[37] Blend, "Mary Austin and the Western Conservation Movement," 14.
[38] Ibid.
[39] "Suffrage Day by Day," *The Washington Herald*, November 29, 1915, 8.
[40] Ibid.
[41] "Cavalry Section in Parade," *Evening Star*, November 30, 1915, 7.
[42] "Girls will Head Suffrage Parade" *The Washington Herald*, November 30, 1915, 2.
[43] Florence E. Yoder, "Peace Will Come Only After Its Dramatic Appeal Has Been Made Equal to War Appeal," *The Washington Times*, December 3, 1915, 12.

journalist Florence Yoder wrote a piece on Mary Hunter Austin's drive to be dramatic until she was heard in the women's cause (previously, Yoder had written about the progressive idea of the "School for Lovers" in 1914).[44] The author's flair for the dramatic continued for as long as she was with the party women (whom she later criticizes), and descriptions of her as being an "expert in pageantry" can be seen in connection with the continuous staging of dramatic parades and suchlike.[45]

In the years to come, Austin became more radical in her activism, and with regard to the themes of her later works (*The Young Woman Citizen* and *No. 26 Jayne Street*), she displays her discomfort with big corporations and questions of citizenship. To support this view, the plots are always heavily set on criticizing capital greed and how it steps on individuals. The story, despite being philosophically charged with activism on both nature and democracy, also lays a strong base for female characters – even if it is meant to follow the maturing process of a male protagonist. It allows the women to excel at whatever they are doing, whether it be fighting for democracy and against capitalism or being strong-willed, hard-working women who stand up for the right to their womanhood. Despite the book being written in 1917, the story does not directly acknowledge anything about the war situation, as it is set in a different time and is inspired by real events. However, *The Ford* draws lines between the social situations unfolding at the time of the book's publication, such as the one linked to cooperate greed and capitalism, and the themes of democracy and demonstrations. The significance given to female characters in the story and the celebration of their achievements is also in many ways impacted by the new gender roles that Austin was experiencing and was not necessarily something that was true of the story of Tierra Longa or the real Owens Valley.

The Young Woman Citizen (1918)

Summary

It is important to note that *The Young Woman Citizen* is not fiction but an important extended political essay written at a critical time when the United States joined the war as an active belligerent. Austin's intent when writing this was to explain in depth her vision of the contributions that women could make to American politics and public life. Summarizing such a book is more about analyzing it rather than just retelling it from page to page. The main

---

[44] Ibid.
[45] "Twelve Women on Horseback," *The Sunday Star*, December 5, 1915, 19.

perspectives and reflections are true Austin's essence and are opinions she had presented earlier, whether it be in the undertones of her fiction or in her daily activism.

Austin writes that the work is dedicated to the young women of America who first assumed their share of political responsibility during the crisis in their country's history in the hope that it may aid them in carrying their citizenship successfully, with as high a sense of privilege and obligation as had supported the women of an earlier generation whose labors won them their opportunity.[46]

In the book, Austin is describing a time in which women were fueled with the desire to be heard and taken seriously in their quest for equality, thus encouraging them to stand up and take their share of responsibility in society/politics. Austin's writing links everything to the First World War, as the war became the breaking point for the women's rights agenda. The book's intentions have been described as an analysis of the obligations of citizenship, which was assumed by both men and women with the right to vote.[47] The book argues for the importance of educated citizenship, and its intentions are a guiding voice for discussions and improvements. It also presents core socialist beliefs and how these can be used in a positive manner to create a closeness of nation and citizens through understanding basic politics and taking part in it as members of society (regardless of gender).

The First World War brought many debates to the agenda, among which was women's share in the democracy that the United States so fiercely believed they were defending by participating in the war. Thus, Austin's contribution has been described as "an admirable discussion of the responsibilities of the new democracy and of woman's [sic] share in it."[48] The mobilization of women because of the war, due to the lack of men present on the home front, had a major effect on motivating the likes of Mary Austin's literature (which ultimately was her occupation).

The effect of the war on literature in general is something that can be read in great detail in *Soldier's Heart: Literary Men, Literary Women, and the Great War* by Sandra M. Gilbert, who discusses how the war, despite its brutality on the battlefield, also 'produced' many great American war poets who later became notable. Among these were men such as Ernest Hemingway (1899-1961) and E. E. Cummings (1894-1962). The effect of the war on literature will be examined in

---

[46] Austin, *The Young Woman Citizen*, [dedication].
[47] "The Young Woman Citizen," *The Sun*, June 16, 1918, 15.
[48] Dorothy Scarborough, "Choices of 'Books and the Book World,'" *The Sun*, December 1, 1918, 11.

more detail later on, as it presents one of the key contributions to changing society as well as being evidence of how the changes in society/politics affected the literary world (exemplified by Austin, among many others).

Writing from the battlefield was quite common. Simultaneously, writers who did not serve in the war were also inspired by it, such as F. Scott Fitzgerald (1896-1940) and William Faulkner (1897-1962). Through understanding the relations between war, society, and the literary developments of the time, we can also understand the development of Mary Austin's literary direction with *The Young Woman Citizen*. The author argues for suffrage within a larger theory of democratic citizenship that re-imagines the gender structure of the national institution and contributes to the processive work toward constructing an inclusive ideal.[49]

As previously mentioned, *The Young Woman Citizen* has no fictional plot but is an attempt to shed light on the benefits that would come as a result of women taking ownership of their significance when they become aware of the value of their citizenship. The novel is unapologetically political and reads like the manifesto of Mary Hunter Austin's political and social beliefs and understandings in her criticism of society while also attempting to show new solutions. The book insists upon females' conscious preparation for citizenship, but the intention is not to dictate but rather to prepare them for and guide them to a working philosophy of what citizenship entitles the female sex with, particularly in the case of having to re-adjust their lives due to American men joining the war in Europe. The book deliberates on the empowerment of women's position as resourceful citizens, as people who are able to bring something practical to society and to the public. The first chapter maps the importance of Americanization and relating young individuals to political trends.

Chapter Two goes further into the civic consciousness and aims to shed light on methods of administration, which carries on in the book to a point where the author speaks about women's organizations as an asset and that women's power goes to waste in many ways: "Before we have tried out the relation of the woman-nature to democracy, we are called upon to establish newer and higher forms of it than we have ever known."[50] Austin wanted to establish a structure in order to shake the foundations of society as she was experiencing it. Another topic that is discussed is the transition from industrialism to commercialism, which was also evident in *The Ford*, written prior to *The Young Woman Citizen*.

---

[49] Gabrielson, "Woman-Thought," 651.
[50] Austin, *The Young Woman Citizen*, 6.

Austin is weary of the condition of workers and argues that "if you find yourself unable to deal with the pattern of labor unionism and [the] nice distinction between Marxian and Fabian Socialism, you can at least determine that the woman who washes your clothes in a laundry shall not do so under any worse conditions than prevail in your own kitchen; or the seamstress who sews for you in a shop be any the less under your eyes and protection."[51]

The writer insists that women can march to the beat of their own drum and argues that the female nature is one of democracy. She writes that men are fighting the war to protect women from other men, or so they like to believe, because women are doing remarkable things regardless of such assumed protection. The book gives descriptions of women holding their husband's place in shops or factories, claiming, "What we women must also hold is the place America has set in the first line of democratic thinking."[52] This means that the empowerment of holding the physical fort up should not be satisfactory in itself but should rather create a hunger to demand the right to hold power politically as well. The example of women's 'manpower' strengthens the conviction that women can in fact prove their fitness for citizenship exactly as they are and as they do things. "For so many centuries man's intelligence was the only kind of intelligence,"[53] the author writes. Her fundamental belief was that the lack of acknowledgment for women in society was out of balance because men's privilege as men had been consistent, with or without war situations, for a long time before she wrote this book; thus, what the book expresses is a series of her opinions throughout the years between 1914 and 1918.[54]

Upon America's entrance into the war, and in the years leading up to her most notable political essays (*The Young Woman Citizen* and "Sex Emancipation,"), Austin is said to have been "for peace, but argues that unless the beauties and fruits of peace are shown [to] the people, and made to the individual, it will not come," because recruitment in such matters is only successful if eagerness is a belief shared by many, much like the belief that "war is the traditional means of expressing the ultimate opinion of the individuals."[55] Austin speaks of how she believes that much like men at war are convinced that their part, whatever it may be, is important, so is the fight

---

[51] Ibid., 168.
[52] Ibid., 9.
[53] Ibid., 16.
[54] Mary Hunter Austin, "Women as Pacifists," *New York Tribune*, February 17, 1917, 8.
[55] Ibid.

for peace because it, too, needs to be dramatized like war.[56] "She claims that the same things which make war popular – drums, music, uniforms marching in line – will make peace popular with the peoples of all nations of the world."[57] This is the exact "moment in history" where Mary Hunter Austin's pacifism can perhaps be determined more than at any other time because, over the years, we see that this pacifism changes in relation to the war.

A notable and interesting thing about the author's presence is that the way in which she was portrayed varied from place to place. For example, in Washington, DC, the news would be promoting her activism relating to the suffrage movement, while in New York, it would be paying more attention to her literary voice of genius, especially around the years of the war's breakout in Europe.[58] Austin's participation in suffrage activities was at its peak during this time, and among her activities were not only luncheons but various voluntary efforts, such as fun activities in parks on the initiative of the Equal Suffrage Publicity Committee.[59] Her activism is observed differently depending on the state in question, and while journalists in New York often focused on announcements of events within the city, quite naturally, as part of the relevant events going on such as suffrage fairs, other journalists elsewhere could write wide-ranging pieces about what they deemed relevant and why. In some places, suffrage affairs were strictly politically intended rather than socially so.

Austin's political drive for women's rights continued in a stronger suit in 1915, and the first mention of her in the press comes on January 5, when the *New York Tribune* announced that she would host a luncheon at the National Arts Club, Gramercy Park, in honor of suffrage.[60] In addition to hosting suffrage luncheons, the writer was also involved in a project regarding suffragists as editors.[61] This was intended as a measure to further the campaign for suffrage. The number of activist women in New York contributing through literary works, such as newspapers and books, grew, and among the publications was a women's edition of *The Sun*.[62] The women's edition was linked to the Empire State Campaign Committee, "which is

---

[56] Ibid.
[57] Ibid.
[58] "Suffragists to Talk at Keith's," *The Washington Herald*, December 6, 1915, 4; "Mrs. Belmot Arrives," *The Washington Times*, December 6, 1915, 4; "Address at Keith's Theater," *The Evening Star*, December 7, 1915, 2; "Suffrage Fair at St. Regis," *The Sun*, December 6, 1914, 8; "One Foot Feats in Aid of Suffrage," *The Sun*, June 27, 1915, 5.
[59] Ibid.
[60] "To Entertain Suffragists," *New York Tribune*, January 5, 1915, 7.
[61] "Suffragists as Editor," *The Sun*, January 8, 1915, 16.
[62] "A Newspaper by Women for Women and Everybody Else," *The Sun*, April 6, 1915, 5.

conducting the fight for Woman Suffrage in New York,"[63] and Austin is mentioned as an editor. She was also cited among the authors who were popular in diverse fields during the second annual dinner of the Authors League of America.[64] Austin is reported to have led an informal discussion on questions of copyright and the ideals of American letters.[65] At this point, one can gather that the writer's significance as a stable and well-informed literary contributor was gaining more validation on big stages.

All of these factors and notices of the author's life and activities were consistent in leading to the publication of *The Young Woman Citizen*, and despite the main component of the book being radical political thinking in matters of citizenship and suchlike, the narrative also contains self-contradictions. This is perhaps more to do with Austin's eclecticism than hypocrisy, but it is worth noting that although she stood by the mainstream idea that WWI was the war to end all wars (to quote Wilson), she also claimed that any movement that thought of itself as an almighty instance of social unrest presents itself as not evolving.[66] Thus, one can interpret this as either evolving with the times or selling out.

In this book, more than in any other, Austin is critical of politics using a direct message; she sheds light on subjects such as free speech and addresses censorship of the being and of freedom of expression. This was relevant during the war period, particularly with regard to the American administration dedicating so much effort to keeping the public in check, using strong claims like "giving the feeling of partnership that comes with full, frank statements concerning the conduct of the public business."[67] This, again, is rather self-contradictory because the US government claimed absolute transparency, yet the truth was filled with propaganda (which Austin later addressed and reflected on in *No. 26 Jayne Street*).

The developing situation in Europe, despite it not concerning the United States until April 1917, made the people contemplate the war, and it became a social-, political- and gender-related agent of change, very strongly so when *The Young Woman Citizen* was published in 1918.[68] To provide a prime example of its socialistic growth and impact, the historian David Kennedy, author of *Over Here: The First World War and American Society* (1980),

---

[63] Ibid.
[64] "Authors Have a Prosperous Year and Big Banquet," *The Sun*, April 17, 1915, 6.
[65] Ibid.
[66] Austin, *The Young Woman Citizen*, 68.
[67] Kennedy, *Over Here*, 60.
[68] Wilson, *New York and the First World War*, 78-80.

describes how "the socialist party was among the first groups to feel the whip of official wrath."[69] As a result of the party's standing as the largest organized center of opposition to American participation in the war, the authorities put bans on social publications in order to dial them down. Kennedy describes this time as a time the socialist movement of American never truly recovered from.[70] This is particularly evident in newspaper articles of the time; for example, an article in the conservative newspaper *The Idaho Republican* directly encouraged people to ask questions to weed out socialists. The general view was that while some of these socialists were native-born Americans, some had also arrived from other countries. The narrative was that these socialist newcomers displayed ungratefulness because they dared to find fault with the United States despite the freedom they had been granted.[71] The general (perhaps uneducated) perception was: "True type Socialists do not believe in Christianity, do not believe in the holy institution of matrimony. Do believe and have incorporated in the Non-partisan platform a tax clause which means that all the improvements and buildings are exempt from taxes and land only is taxed."[72] The red-blooded American was to think of socialists and socialism as ungrateful lawbreakers and fornicators. This view from *The Idaho Republican* from October 1918 shows how the rebellious and radical movement, which Austin was advocating, was considered from a conservative perspective. This gives an idea about how far the distance between the political left and right was, even at a time when the United States was going full force on promoting national unity and brotherhood to fight German autocracy and maintain American democracy.[73]

The scholar Sandra Adickes describes New York during the early 1900s, up to the war, as a time and gathering point for liberals, anarchists, and socialists; in short, "revolutionists of all shades."[74] Manhattan was the place where those who were different in society, artists and the likes of Austin, met and evolved in union. It was an optimistic time for women because they gathered at this physical and mental 'meeting point' in the heart of New York.[75] Thus, the setting is symbolic and true to reality. The series of arguments in the book make logical sense (subjectively in a socialist narrative) because they ultimately prove women as a wholesome resource – not as 'second class members' of society, but

---

[69] Kennedy, *Over Here*, 26-27.
[70] Ibid.
[71] "Mr. Farmer, are you afraid to investigate?" *The Idaho Republican*, October 22, 1918, 8.
[72] Ibid.
[73] Kennedy, *Over Here*, 70.
[74] Adickes, *To Be Young Was Very Heaven*, 2-3.
[75] Ibid., 4-5.

a whole contributing foundation alongside men. Women had to peacefully become a valuable and equal resource in such critical times of chaos, particularly in chaos that was orchestrated by men. Adickes goes on to argue that America needed to establish practical relationships with the world as a whole, instead of trying to impose itself on the different nations, to set aside arrogance in order to avoid wars and conflicts.

Among the very important and overall messages Austin conveys is that, up to the beginning of the war, all existent political tensions centered on the relation between capital and labor, which confirms the undertones that she presented in the symbolism of her works in this period (e.g. *The Ford*).[76] The overall message of her political essay is directly linked to her belief that labor, regardless of gender, is what made society strong in every aspect of its existence (politically, socially, economically, etc.). Although she was not a practical woman, having no real academic or political education, the ideas she continued pushing toward mobilization were in equal parts social and political.[77] She references simple acts such as unification through similar dress codes, such as those the men of "successful working-men's union[s]" wore to meetings. [78] She wanted to promote unity as citizens, as workers, as women, and as Americans because she believed what made America weak was the lack of correlation between all the forces within the nation.

Austin concludes that faith in the common experience of the sex is the best thing that women could bring to the political arena, despite the ongoing war; she deems it crucial that women be seen as important in the effort to win the war in order to be taken seriously as part of building a new world. In order to achieve political education, one must search for simplification, which one is to find in art, science, and history. If the mentioned search is too hard for one to understand, then one must simply continue in one's pursuit because the common process of living and seeking creative solutions is how one sustains life as a woman.

Historians have confirmed that, despite the lack of the United States' involvement in the earlier years of the global conflict, the matter of building identity and anxieties about citizenship were flourishing.[79] This helps to explain the presence of the political debate and subject matter of Austin's second book. In many ways, *The Young Woman Citizen* is what laid the basis for Austin to continue her ideologies and vision into the truth-based fiction of

---

[76] Austin, *The Young Woman Citizen*, 160-161.
[77] Ibid., 162-164.
[78] Ibid., 133.
[79] Wilson, *New York and the First World War*, 15.

No. 26 Jayne Street – as well as taking the fiction from *The Ford* and adapting it into a more direct philosophical message about the future, instead of a censored fictional one based on prior experience.

The Young Woman Citizen struggled financially post-publication, as well as pre-publication, because it was not cost-efficient to print right away. People were not in a place where they had the luxury of buying such books, despite the drive of the 'radical' females in society being very present. However, the book became of value years after its publication and after the end of the war, for example by being used to teach both men and women the importance of using their voice and vote. Thus, the book was used as a teaching example because it was described as a "penetrating analysis of the obligations of citizenship which are assumed by men and women with the wish to vote."[80] The gender aspects of the book were applicable at this time because the women's movement, both in its pacifist radicalism, its anti-war movements, as well as its suffrage efforts to secure what later became the Nineteenth Amendment in 1920, aimed to ensure that gendered prejudice would be outlawed.[81]

However, perhaps one of the main reasons why this book might have flopped in a way was its weak practical notions, as one of the weakest points in the book is Austin's lack of background in practical politics; she focuses more on the correlations between the spiritual and the practical and so on.[82] Clearly, there is a passion, there is a mindset, and there is a vision, however it lacks any real practical approach on exactly how to tackle the political themes it presents. This dilemma was often present for Austin, who had no problem with speaking to large audiences of important men because she was a passionate soul, but she was not always a politically practical one. Austin discusses how every aspect of America is connected but that there is an imbalance; thus, "woman-thinking" should start at the nearest point (e.g. children).[83]

Perhaps why the book did not hit a larger audience is because it was woman-thought, meaning it examines, tosses, and turns over problems, but it stands alone. The book is a political essay, but it would have been a great manifesto with more success if it had been a joint effort between politicians, doctors, economists, parks and recreation representatives, etc. joining forces to find actual ways to turn Austin's vision into a practicable science. The book is clever

---

[80] "The Cornerstone of Citizenship! To be Published in July The Young Woman Citizen by Mary Austin," *The Sun,* June 16, 1918, 15.
[81] Adickes, *To Be Young Was Very Heaven,* 98-100.
[82] Austin, *The Young Woman Citizen,* 20.
[83] Ibid., 21-22.

for its time, presenting the idea that World Democracy must be committed to like religion because democracy and spiritual faith are the same.[84]

"Sex Emancipation Through War" (1918)

Summary

Perhaps more successful than *The Young Woman Citizen* was Austin's short political essay "Sex Emancipation Through War," published in 1918.[85] This essay, if nothing else, is a direct feminist work, even if it might not have been called as such. In the essay, Austin writes that the world was in the habit of thinking that it is women only who were in need of sex emancipation, however she deemed that it was in fact only women who were clever enough to know that they needed it because men did too. She suggested that men were so wrapped up and tied into their sex that most of them did not know that this was a disorderly structure.

The essay tackles the issues of women's work, and the long-standing lack thereof, and how it has been underestimated. She continues to write that what the war will ultimately come to and needs sorely more than anything else – more than religion, democracy, civilization, and so on – is "sex emancipation." The idea is presented as undoubtedly certain, to the point that she believes that the war will not end until sex emancipation is achieved: "anything we can accomplish toward that emancipation will have its share in bringing the war to an end."

Men think that the political world is a male place that women have broken into by not wholly fortunate accident and which they can only stay within by becoming, in some fantastic way, unwomanly, unsexed. Men are so gorged and saturated with sex, as sex may be expressed in social conditions, that they think of this war as cataclysmic, made in Germany or in Hell, or anywhere except where it actually is, in the very center of male consciousness, and made there only by virtue of our not being able to see it as an exhibition of masculinity run amuck. The literary approach in this article is one of the most scientific of Austin's works, despite her flair for dramatics that influenced her writing. She presents statistics, but she also writes the text in a way that makes reading it feel like going through a letter to a friend.

Austin conveys the discussion of how it is but a superstition that the work a human being does or may do is determined by sex. Secondly, she argues

---

[84] Ibid., 25.
[85] Austin, *Beyond Borders*, 44-55.

against the social value of a woman being established by what some man thinks of her and how it is utterly ridiculous that the man alone must 'support' the family. Austin's advocacy for the war is clearly shown as she argues that the war was there to save womankind (as much as women will save the war) because it came in time to "save us endless agonies of doubt and discussion as to whether women have strength enough, or brains enough, for the four hundred and fifty-seven callings which war has added to those already open to women."[86]

The essay discusses the author's belief that there are "probably" ineradicable differences between the abilities of the two sexes, but that the war is a good thing because it has demonstrated that the differences are not the traditional distinctions of superior and inferior; for example, there are no actual different *kinds* of ability required for handling a telephone switchboard, etc., a task that had traditionally been handed to women, and as such positions such as train dispatching also did not require skills related to one's biological sex, although the social norm used to indicate as such.[87] The difference, Austin believed, was in "quality" and the personal ability to produce a steady quality of attention for given periods in various jobs, meaning that, "in other words, it is not so much brains as nervous stability that is required."[88] The essay is not critical of war, nor is it hateful toward men, nor does it attempt to discredit any gender; what it does is establish that women are capable and that the jobs allowing the room for women to work in traditionally non-female positions are proof of this capability that women already know they possess but are never allowed to demonstrate. Austin writes that women themselves have always known that "nervousness," leading to doubt in their capabilities because of hysteria and nervousness and other assumptions, is not a biological sex trait.[89] Modern feminism as its own entity aside, this political essay is more about equality of function than feminism in its intellectuality; however, since feminism is a matter of equality, ultimately this is a feminist piece of writing as much as anything else. Austin continues her flair for dramatics as she contends that any nervousness that women must have is fair game because men were probably nervous themselves when the world war was a comparatively unknown place.[90] Despite her dramatic antics, she also refers to scientific finds related to female health and believes that the view of

---

[86] Austin, "Sex Emancipation," 46.
[87] Ibid., 49.
[88] Ibid.
[89] Ibid.
[90] Ibid.

capability based on sex should progress alongside everything else modern. The idea is that there is no history of the development of an indication that a woman has no value to society except that which man gives her as the object of his desire and the mother of his children; it has simply grown out of man's nature.[91] Men have always had a history of believing themselves martyrs for the sake of womanhood, waging wars and such, yet they do not step aside for women to step up and excel in matters of architecture, biology, sociology, and so on because a woman's contribution is only as good as it can be as long it does not overstep a *man's* contribution.[92] Modern feminism is a drive for equality, and although this was also the case for Austin, she could come off as rather hostile to make her points, based on statements such as "men have never hesitated to take a woman out of society and insist that every gift, every possible contribution of hers to general human welfare shall be excised, aborted, done with."[93] Maybe a valid conclusion as to why Austin was not recognized as a great feminist voice of her own until much later is because of this particular criticism, perhaps even aggression, in her methods, which were too rigid for the mainstream of her time.

Further on, the norm prior to the changes that came with the war was rather shameful in that waged female workers were discarded at around thirty-five years of age, which was on average ten years younger than male workers as the women begin to exhaust themselves and expire, which often left the women with less confidence in their abilities and position as they were discardable.[94]

Analysis

This essay is undoubtedly a political and 'feminist' one, and it was absolutely inspired by and dedicated to the way in which women could an equal asset to men. The narrative clearly shows Austin's position as a strong frontier-fighter for social change in her time, particularly through work and response to conflict. It was perhaps motivated by her self-sufficiency as a woman who had provided for herself and her child alone. She firmly writes that work resulting in a sudden reversal of ideas about work and women is one of the greatest wonders of civilization thus far.[95] Women's need for emancipation was not a foreign concept in Austin's literary work, and almost all analysis of her writing

---

[91] Ibid., 50.
[92] Ibid.
[93] Ibid.
[94] Ibid., 51.
[95] Ibid.

eventually leads to one central demand: women will only be free once they can provide for themselves. Work would ensure safety because, ultimately, the social structures in society were all undoubtedly made to serve men. "Sex Emancipation Through War" is not angry in its tone, but firm. It is a plea for change and an observation of flaws, in which one can hear Austin trying to wake up her fellow females. The economic exploitation of women was something not everyone was aware of, and if they were, they simply ignored it. Thus, Austin, perhaps somewhat dramatically for a Christian woman, claimed it 'superstition' that the quality of work was determined by the biological sex. The social and intellectual women should not be established by what men thought them to be. The time was right for a single woman like Austin to make such strong statements in which she directly criticized family structures, work ethics, and society's flaws. She was not labeled a crazy woman but an advocate, and that was because the times were changing and the stage was ready for her political outbursts in the form of literary pleas. The time was right to stand by the idea that labor would ensure freedom.

When linking this essay to *The Young Woman Citizen*, it becomes clear how her ideas intertwine; in order to claim one's citizenship fully, work is freedom and freedom is the gain of one's emancipation and citizenship. The author debates further that the basic prejudice against women in the world's work positions has been more about not providing them with good working conditions and waged work than being against them actually working. The reason, according to Austin, was that women working was fundamental in the obscurity of their own homes, which was deemed of "social unimportance," but it was dull and heavy labor requiring little more than brute strength. Spending the amount of energy women actually spend on providing food for tens of working hands in the fields is no less hard work or ladylike than any other occupation.

Austin believed that women saw the world differently, and in "Woman-Thought, Social Capital, and the Generative State: Mary Austin and the Integrative Civic Ideal in Progressive Thought,"[96] Teena Gabrielson reflects on Austin's definition of women's second characteristics (and their importance). This 'second characteristic' is women's intuitive judgment, "a way of seeing the world rather than just maternal instincts or feelings,"[97] about which Austin is quoted as saying, "At any rate, it is the woman habit to think the next thing which enables women to keep their opinion in [a] continuous state of

---

[96] Gabrielson, "Woman-Thought," 656.
[97] Ibid.

mobilization without any suspicious inconsistency."[98] Gabrielson deems Austin's approach to men to be more rigid than that toward the female sex. The gender approach is one that favors women because the female way of thinking is less problematic when attempting to approach particular goals.[99]

Austin claimed that the world was really a very feminine place, a mother's place, conceptive, brooding, nourishing, a place of infinite patience and infinite elusiveness. Thus, the world needed to be lived in more or less femininely, and the chief reason why we have never succeeded in being quite at home in it is that our method has been almost exclusively masculine. An article in *The Chicago Eagle* from May of 1918 deliberates on the writer, stating that "Mary Austin hails the 'sex emancipation of women,' as a result of the war, and presents some of the psychological and emotional problems of the new era of women's independence."[100] The article does not go into any further detail on Austin other than that particular quote, yet it can be linked to *The Young Woman Citizen* and the general perception of Austin's socialist activities.

It is abundantly clear that Austin put a lot of research into her work, which strengthened her political essays. She writes that a clear case and example of the emancipation of industry from the waste of sex prejudice comes from Ohio, where it was discovered that women's instinctive fear of machinery could be turned into an advantage. She points to a case in which it had been made clear that a woman being in charge of overhead cranes led to fewer accidents because women took fewer risks. Austin states that the male ego, in such positions, leads to a loss in lives because they take unnecessary risks that put people in danger, concluding that "it is quite enough for our purpose to know that the woman operator is sufficiently afraid of the mechanism she handles not to be afraid to stop the machinery when there is a question of risk."[101]

And it is as such, and she makes cases and points about how and why women experience the world differently. They do not wish to be men; they wish to exist as women in a public space and provide new female perspectives in old arenas – this is not an override of motherhood, but a breaking of the idea that "man is the norm." Austin's discussion is on how women moving toward emancipation will also provide benefits in terms of ending war; she believed that female emancipation would end war, as the equal co-existence of the sexes could benefit society greatly.[102] If we draw some parallels, we can

---

[98] Ibid.
[99] Ibid.
[100] "The May Forum," *Chicago Eagle*, May 11, 1918, 5.
[101] Austin, "Sex Emancipation," 48.
[102] Austin, *Beyond Borders*, 44.

get an idea of what the author wished for, namely self-awareness, because true self-awareness was not to be achieved until the efforts of both men and women were equally valued, and it becomes clear in the passage that Austin is speaking about both men and women because her perception of sex includes both sexes.

It was a common habit, and perhaps is to this day, to assume that it is only women who were in need of sex emancipation when in fact this was the case for both sexes: "it is only women who are clever enough to know that they need it. Men are so wrapped and swaddled and tied into their sex that most of them don't know yet, that this is not the natural order of things."[103] It takes self-awareness to acknowledge that politics was a male-dominated arena and that breaking into this patriarchal hierarchy would result in women only being allowed to stay if they became "unwomanly and unsexed."[104] The prejudice of women being less womanly if they took up a non-typical female space is something that comes up for discussion from several points of view in the present study, as many individuals in Austin's time claimed. The blame game was evident in other literature and in attitudes as well, for example in David H. Lawrence's "Eloi, Eloi, Lama Sabachthani" (1915), in which writing takes up the sexual anxiety of the Great War and an anger directed toward women, "as if the Great War itself were primarily a climactic episode in some battle of the sexes that had already been raging for years."[105]

Life after the war became what it is because society was different, as was Mary Hunter Austin. The First World War created enormous armies on both sides and was, according to Gilbert, a war classified as virtually completing the Industrial Revolution's construction of anonymity and dehumanization of the man. The war created faceless victims, and the actual violence and killing distanced the people from each other because there was only the soldiers and the no-man's-land between them (each of them thinking of the other as the enemy).[106]

This reflection of a space between the two is perhaps also what we see as the divide between men and women: on the battlefield, there were men, and the land between them created anonymity and made it easier for them to kill each other, while in society this divide was between the two genders. Biological sex was the land that created this distance between the two. The distance between politicians and the people, between the soldiers on the battlefield,

---

[103] Ibid.
[104] Ibid.
[105] Sandra M. Gilbert, "Soldier's Heart: Literary Men, Literary Women, and the Great War," *Signs* 8, no. 3 (1983): 424.
[106] Ibid., 422-424.

between the soldiers and their home, between men and women, etc. are all notable and topics of discussion because as much as the distance was evident in practice, it was also symbolic in all arenas.

Gilbert discusses how the no-man's-land between the man and the enemy (subjectively) was not just symbolic for the machinery of death and the new technological way of killing, it was also a symbol for the state, which man is powerless to control or protest against. The literature was now evidently portraying the effects of war in its tales, symbols, and metaphors.[107] There was a new self-awareness about the torment between the so-called assault by the bureaucracy and the lethality of technocracy; thus, man becomes "an inhabitant of the inhumane new era and a citizen of the unpromising new land," into which man is led by war.[108] The parodies of war portrayed in the literature by men were also in many ways parodies of sexuality and possibly of female conquest, and women started seeing the distance between themselves and men that had existed earlier; however, they saw it more clearly now that there was a specific geographical distance as well.[109] The reason for this realization came with how the events that took place had different meanings for people based on their gender, and the war put "a barrier of indescribable experience between men and the women whom they loved... Quite early I realised [the] possibility of a permanent impediment to understanding."[110]

The bitterness of women is one thing; however, the bitterness of men was evidently quite another because the idea that the war could possibly be the fault of wives, mothers, daughters, etc. was apparent because they were safe at home and, thus, the "war to end all wars" became somewhat blamed on them as it was subjectively believed they came out of it much safer. Gilbert asks the question of whether "the war appears in some peculiar sense their fault, a ritual of sacrifice to their victorious femininity?" This we can also link to the idea that all wars have habitually been viewed as a destruction of masculinity, leading to "an apotheosis of femaleness."[111]

---

[107] Ibid., 423.
[108] For further reading on topics regarding the psychological consequences for men, see Paul Fussell, *The Great War and Modern Memory* (New York: Oxford University Press, 1975); Eric Leed, *No Man's Land: Combat and Identity in World War I* (New York: Cambridge University Press, 1979).
[109] Gilbert, "Soldier's Heart," 424.
[110] Ibid., 425. For further reading, see Vera Brittain, *Testament of Youth* (London: Fontana/Virago, 1979), 143.
[111] Ibid., 424.

Finally, and upon close consideration of the previously discussed points, one must ask the bigger question about the relations between men and women during this "war to end all wars" in the actual time it unfolded. These questions are meant to be answered in their respective times and not through our modern retrospective view. Consequently, among the questions that have been asked in this research several times before is the following: What part did women play in the war, and how did men comprehend their role? Obviously, this has been answered multiple times to different degrees; however, in the contemporary literary tone, we get other ideas than those of our modern perception. Questions like this started to come up in the literature affected by the war, and it is this that Gilbert's "Soldier's Heart" captures so well.

Looking at the connection between the activities of women in wartime and the damage men felt they were going through gives many answers as to how the change in gender roles came about. The question of whether women themselves experienced the wounds of the war in the same way as their sons and lovers can be answered with the simple response that it depends on the woman. The radical women of New York, such as Austin, Goldman, Jordan, etc., probably experienced it in a completely different way to a non-educated woman from the Midwest.[112]

A key element which Austin understood, and which modern scholars such as Kennedy have determined, was that women running society while men were away would not last, nor would it be the new full-time norm; as she wrote, "some of the freedom gained by this war will have to be surrendered at the end of it."[113] Amongst the points she presents is that of underestimating that there should be no fear by anti-feminists of women doing traditionally male-dominated jobs. Austin, perhaps a little misogynistically per the modern definition and only as 'feminist' as her time allowed, concludes that women doing men's jobs would not ruin their femininity.[114]

Austin concludes with her main apprehensions that the war had helped lift taboos on sex aptitudes and that manpower is a work of social evil (meaning a biased social construction/prejudice). She believed wholeheartedly that at the end of the war, the world would have to face the normal demands of women for marriage and children, which is why they would go back to the old ways; however, it was too early to determine any set numbers of how many would continue their new lives as labor women.

---

[112] Ibid.
[113] Austin, "Sex Emancipation," 52.
[114] Ibid.

The author, although hopeful, was aware that women would never be fully emancipated from the facts of sex but could do something about the way in which they dealt with them. This can be interpreted as encouragement of the 'if you can't beat them, join them' adage, starting by changing the way women reacted to the differences caused by a lack of emancipation.

No. 26 Jayne Street (1920)

No. 26 Jayne Street was written and published in 1920, two years after the First World War had ended, however the plot of the story describes the time leading up to the American interference in the global conflict. The plot, much like Austin's previous publications, speaks of social and political manners and beliefs through a fictional story. The book gives an insight into Austin's growing values in the realm of politics, her stand on war, as well as her ideas about gender and equal marriage. Blanche H. Gelfant writes that Austin infused her novels with feminist messages because she herself "marched in support of women's rights"[115] and "spoke at public rallies,"[116] and thus it draws much from her personal life, her observations, as well as her imagination. The story dabbles heavily in issues of socialism, gender, and war, and the main character can be described as the embodiment of female activists in the years between 1914 and 1920. The *New York Tribune* described the work as one that "conjures up again the intellectual and emotional experiences of the early days of the war."[117]

Matters of equal marriage was a topic Austin had long discussed; in 1914, the advertising-free Chicago daily newspaper *The Day Book* (1911-1917) published a piece called "By and About Women," which examined how England had seventeen schools that, in addition to teaching domestic science, also taught gardening, poultry raising, beekeeping, farming, and horticulture. The article feeds into Austin's stance on marriage being an act of necessity and meaning more to women than to men because women were bound to find husbands in order to prosper "in all her spiritual progressions with processes of physical reorganization. Love in man may change his relation to society, but in woman it changes the woman."[118] This can be read as her wish to progress and for American society to follow suit in helping to support the

---

[115] Gelfant, "'Lives' of Women Writers," 77.
[116] Ibid.
[117] "26 Jayne Street; Greenwich Village at War Pictured by Mary Austin," *New York Tribune*, August 8, 1920, 11.
[118] "By and About Women," *The Day Book*, June 5, 1914, 20.

development of women toward not being so marriage-bound.[119] Austin's opinion on domestic affairs was respected because of the themes of her writing, and perhaps personal experiences, as can be read in New York newspapers. However, it was not only in progressive New York that the knowledgeable socialist was consulted on her views but also in Chicago. *The Day Book* refers to Austin's philosophy in *Love and the Soul Maker* (1914) and quotes the author saying that

> ...mate love does not always imply parental love; that romantic passion between men and women is not merely a nature's preface to fatherhood and motherhood but is the oldest need and strongest instinct of the human race. She says that mate love, the love of one man for one woman existed in a past so dim that parenthood was looked upon as a miracle, utterly detached from the sex relation and in no way a consequence of it. 'Marriage,' as Mrs. Austin defines it, 'is an agreement between any pair to practice mate love toward one another with intention.'[120]

Summary

The book is about twenty-six-year-old Neith Schuyler, who is from an old and aristocratic New York family and who returns to the United States after a ten-year period of living with her father in Europe, namely in Italy and France, as the conflict in Europe kicked into high gear. Neith's father has passed away, and so she returns alone to her old aunts. Despite being from a rich and upper-class family, the main protagonist seeks independence by deciding to live in an apartment, No. 26 on Jayne Street, instead of in the rich suburbs. She gives up the lavish life she could have had and instead seeks simplicity. Her main guardians are her older aunts, who are responsible for her, but Neith breaks the barrier about "all sorts of silly notions about what unmarried women can or cannot do."[121]

The plot follows different events that took place in the days before the war, such as worker strikes and peace rallies, but it is mainly Austin's recollection of events that happened in the previous years. The book provides an amalgamation of a love story and an intensely political plot. Neith becomes politically active in the radical movements of New York and participates in

---

[119] Ibid.
[120] "Mary Austin Discovers Love-Grafters – 'Birds of Speckled Feathers,'" *The Day Book*, June 10, 1914, 10.
[121] Austin, *No. 26 Jayne Street*, 46.

strikes and demonstrations. Throughout the story, she meets two potential love interests. The first is Eustace Rittenhouse, who is an 'all-American boy' who eventually goes to war and dies, fulfilling the role of someone fighting for democracy. The second is Adam Frear, a radical revolutionary socialist whom everyone in the community idolizes. Adam's former lover, Rose Matlock, comes along with him into the story as the 'other woman.'

The main storyline ultimately revolves around both men asking Neith to marry them, but she is skeptical despite developing feelings for both. On the one hand, a partnership with Eustace could potentially just be a marriage of convenience and a rather traditional one in which she is a homemaker. On the other hand, Adam is radical but is still not one for an equal partnership in a marriage, which also creates an imbalance in her pull toward choosing him. In regard to her relationship with Adam, Neith comes to realize that he is not as progressive in love as he is in politics and the novel ends with her returning his ring, thus ending their short-lived engagement. Despite taking a stand against masculinity by rejecting Adam, the story ends with Neith's heart still beating for him, hoping he will come back willingly. Despite this longing, she enters a new phase of her life: walking through different places in the city, alone, where once she had walked with Adam, she thinks about her part in the new social revolution. Despite the absence of love, there is something new (and optimistic) in the air.

Analysis

The story is a take on the radical movement in the heart of New York. One love interest, Adam, represents what looks like radical thinking and fearlessness, but he is in many ways a satirical description of utopianism. This particular idealistic hope was not unknown to Austin's character, as her ideologies were often hard to follow through, and according to Dr. Blend, Austin's views often seemed impractical to the bureaucracy.[122] On the other end of the scale in the story is Eustace, who represents willing action and is the symbol of all the men who went to war. He goes into battle fearlessly, which awakens a drive in Neith that makes her question politics that are only words and never actions. The two men are the two sides of American society and politics during the war: the pacifists and the fighters of bloody battles.

In the story, Neith is said to be "New to the Social Revolution"[123] upon her return to New York, and the reader can follow her observation of society and

---

[122] Blend, "Mary Austin and the Western Conservation Movement," 21-22.
[123] Austin, *No. 26 Jayne Street*, 68.

the lack of concern she detects in her fellow Americans, who are oblivious and not troubled with the situation in Europe. This was in fact the exact projection of society, as the war was viewed as exotic and too far away to be a real concern.[124] The main character's life in New York becomes one consumed by politics, starting with her attendance at a strike for workers' rights. This was a direct reflection of the real-life conditions unfolding in the time period for workers in Seattle and, later, police in Boston, etc.; the high demands of the war had been hard on the Pacific Northwest shipbuilding and lumbering industries, leading to negative developments for the workers, who experienced housing shortages and high prices.[125] The government was exploiting the workers to such an extent, going against everything the unions stood for, that workers walked out because the unions promised to keep the basic utilities going.[126] This was not a one-off – it was a repeated occurrence in the critical periods of the war.

The public's acts of disobedience increased because people were unhappy with the conditions, and other workers were encouraged to follow suit. For example, a nationwide steelworkers' strike took place. In addition to this, there were threats of potential further strikes, for instance a coal operators' strike that was directly ordered by Vladimir Lenin (1870-1924) and Leon Trotsky (1879-1940).[127] The House of Representatives showed its lack of tolerance for radicals by refusing to seat an elected Socialist Representative from Wisconsin.[128]

Trotsky, the Russian revolutionary, is also an important character, fictionalized in the novel.[129] He is someone Adam deems a real revolutionary, being more on board with the radical development of the unfolding Russian Revolution than even Neith was aware of (to begin with).[130] Further on, the novel is directly descriptive of the time when American women were left at the home front while the conflict in Europe grew, eventually including America, due to which, as Austin writes, "mortification was in the air. Politicians, the Press, rushed about making the early republican gestures of patriotism and world Democracy. There were bands and banners. None of which quite

---

[124] Wilson, *New York and the First World War*, 44.
[125] Kennedy, *Over Here*, 288-290.
[126] Ibid., 288.
[127] Ibid., 289.
[128] Ibid., 290.
[129] Austin, *No. 26 Jayne Street*, 105.
[130] Ibid.

concealed from the honest..."[131] This was the case with Woodrow Wilson and his administration's campaign, which was one based on promoting the war as a democratic struggle against German autocracy, and thus the people lived in such conditions.[132]

With regard to issues of gender, in the time before entering the war, Neith joined a peace meeting attended by "thirty-five to forty women,"[133] and she recalls: "The Voluntary parenthood lady proposed a universal strike of women not to bear children until the war was abolished."[134] Motherhood as a tool in warfare is very interesting, and Austin using this in her literature is wholesome to say the least because the idealism of motherhood was either seen as the force of female activists, where the usage of the concept of motherhood was used in rhetoric, or an image of the motherly, such as the one Theodore Roosevelt (1858-1919) used when he said: "The woman must bear and rear the children as her first duty to the state," lest "the whole social system collapse."[135] Thus, to use such dialogue in her work is powerful, despite the letdown of knowing that the problematic element at the time was that those who fought for women, for example the National Congress of Mothers, were devoted to maternal ideas, not actual gender equality. Both David Kennedy and Sandra Adickes reflect on this by saying that different women's groups had different intentions, and perhaps the Women's Suffragette Movement was the more well-mannered one compared to other, more radical branches in the gender fight.[136]

In true Austin nature, her books contain a male character who is unintentionally misogynistic, in this case, Adam, despite him being portrayed as progressive. The character seems revolutionary but lacks understanding/ support for the opposite sex, which makes Neith feel less keen on a union with him. The scholar Janis Stout writes that "in the more complex structure of *No. 26 Jayne Street* it is less clear that Neith Schuyler's soundly feminist refusal to accept Adam Frear's disregard of women's rights in his private

---

[131] Ibid., 159.
[132] Kennedy, *Over Here*, 70.
[133] Ibid., 123.
[134] Ibid., 124.
[135] Stacy Alaimo, "The Undomesticated Nature of Feminism: Mary Austin and the Progressive Women Conservationists," *Studies in American Fiction* 26, no. 1 (1998): 73-96.
[136] Adickes, *To Be Young Was Very Heaven*, 89. For further reading on women's suffrage and women's war work, see Laura Lee Downs, "War Work," in *The Cambridge History of the First World War Civil Society*, vol. 3, ed. Jay Winter (Cambridge: Cambridge University Press, 2014), 72-95.

morality brings her satisfaction or fulfillment."[137] In this work, we can get a deeper understanding of Austin's eclectic nature and paradoxical traits. Stout's judgment goes into a discussion about how the writer's feminism is in many ways contradictory. Among the factors that might be judgmental are the continuous desire for equality, the desire to maintain the motherly, as well as the continuing wish to be empowered while also having deeper roots in religion. In the case of Mary Hunter Austin, her religious belonging or spiritual journey only increased alongside her activism, which to many seems self-contradictory; however, one does not exclude the other, and the effects of this development will be discussed later on. Stout firmly argues that Austin rebelled against the status of women in a way that was entirely based on Austin's empirical and naturalistic defense of the matter, even labeling herself as a "fighting feminist" in the later years of her life.[138]

The 'anti-female' sentiment within the socialist movement can once again be linked to this point. Miller writes that, on issues linked to gender, a close look at the Socialist Party revealed that, despite the endorsement of inclusion and equal rights, the leaders and the majority of party members displayed no real interest in its gender policy. The party failed on program promotions, nor did it ever actively encourage female recruitment.[139] However, women still joined the party, and it was these individuals who promoted the female-friendly policies despite the segregation within the actual party.[140] The optimistic times, described by Adickes as the birth of a new spirit, are perhaps what blinded so many to settle for this radicalism, described as a "religion without a name."[141]

One can without any doubt identify Austin in her main character, Neith, as both had experience from their stays in Europe that colored their perspective on the American standard as shallow if nothing else. The book, and probably Austin's own experience, was described as a discovery of decadent aristocracy and exotic radicalism "with an admixture of the nouveau-riche successful business man [sic]."[142] These tropes, i.e. the radicals, the aristocrats, etc., that Austin used were helpful in voicing American opinions on the war and her own need to explore all aspects of the war through different characters. Analytically, it is rather evident that the inspirations for these ideas came from

---

[137] Stout, "Mary Austin's Feminism," 77-101.
[138] Ibid., 77.
[139] Miller, "For White Men Only," 285.
[140] Ibid.
[141] Adickes, *To Be Young Was Very Heaven*, 11.
[142] Ibid.

the author's own escapades, e.g. the years spent in New York City after her travels in Europe were exactly of the sort that one is to read in her fiction. Austin came to befriend the wealthy connoisseur and supporter of the arts Mabel Dodge Luhan, who arranged for evening gatherings at her 23 Fifth Avenue Apartment.[143] The people whom Austin came to meet at these gatherings included socialists, various journalists, trade unionists, anarchists, artists, clubwomen, suffragists, poets, psychoanalysts, and so on,[144] all of whom clearly are the people inspiring (and leading to the spiraling of) these tales. It is no surprise that her social criticism would grow on the pages of her books when her social circle included the Russian Jewish anarchist, Emma Goldman, known to many as "the high priestess of anarchy,"[145] and her lover Alexander Berkman (1870-1936).[146] As mentioned, the author never separated her truth and life from her art, and analyzing anything she wrote is essentially a retelling of her life story. In the company of some of society's most radical individuals, building relations across class and ideologies is above all else what led the author to write stories such as *No. 26 Jayne Street*: "She tells where society lives, who are the leaders in the radical set, and so on."[147] Most of Austin's works have in later years been selected by scholars as being culturally significant and key in the cultivation of intellectual knowledge; her books place fiction in historical contexts that are important for both history and literature and are deemed of great value and nuance in the telling of the story of modern civilization. The works' literary values are as political criticisms and post-war reflections because the author wrote what she knew.

No. 26 Jayne Street was described upon its publication as "a novel which strikes at the very root of special privilege,"[148] and "neither suffrage nor prohibition nor economic independence nor bobbed hair nor any scheme of justice avails unless the Junker in man is exorcised."[149] The Village plays a key role in developing Neith's attempts to make something grand out of her

---

[143] Fink, *I-Mary*, 167-168.
[144] Ibid., 168.
[145] Jeffrey A. Johnson, "Aliens, Enemy Aliens, and Minors: Anti-Radicalism and the Jewish Left," in *Historicizing Fear: Ignorance, Vilification, and Othering*, eds. Travis D. Boyce and Winsome M. Chunnu (Boulder, CO: University Press of Colorado, 2020), 200.
[146] Emily Hahn, *Mable* (New York: Houghton Mifflin Company, 1977), 67-71. For further reading on notable individuals in New York at that time, see Emily Hahn, *Romanic Rebels: An Informal History of Bohemianism in America* (New York: Houghton Mifflin Company, 1967).
[147] J.C.L, "No. 26 Jayne Street," *The New Republic*, October 6, 1920, 152.
[148] Ibid., 151.
[149] Ibid.

understandings of the war situation and the state of society, which reflects on Austin's understanding of social theory. In addition to the social reflection aspects of the book, there is the love and heartbreak in it; Neith wholeheartedly accepts Adam's ideas concerning both society and politics, which sets her up for disappointment because this then creates the expectation of an idealistic marriage, Austin's mate-love narrative (i.e. equal partnership). The disappointment she comes to face in the downfall of this relationship and Adam's shortcoming is not that of being let down by a man, but more the sadness for the woman before her: Rose.[150] In reality, the bond of feminism that Rose and Neith share is much stronger than one Neith might have shared with Adam if they had married, because the imbalance of their sexes is ultimately unavoidable.

> The Feminism of Rose and Neith is more destructive of Junker government and family authority than the battle-cries [sic] of Marx or the suffrage amendment. Rose, with the circumlocutions of the logical mind, and Neith, with instinctive directness, sweep aside the glitter and fascination of cure-alls, demand honest dealing between man and man, man and woman, and woman and woman. They make this fair dealing the requirement for the gift of their love.[151]

The book was described in its own time as ruthless and merciless in its revelation of man's (Adam's) arrogance and women's hopes and desires, but critically also "over-accented," because although it was true that there were many disappointing characters (from Neith's subjective perspective), it is almost arrogant of Austin to write it in a way which makes Neith the only one of her age to have the self-awareness that only a heroine is to possess.[152]

The novel is one heavily infused by love and courtship and the American belief that the nation's role in the world is fighting for democracy, that the world is looking to them, yet many of them (particularly men) seem to lack a deeper understanding of the words they are speaking. Parallel to the embodiment of opposite ideologies within the characters of the main men, the females of the story display similar contrasts as they often display two general positions in life: to affirmingly support the war or to be a revolutionary who (ironically) fights it. The parallel between the men and women of the story therefore resembles a choice in the main character's life:

---

[150] Ibid.
[151] Ibid., 152.
[152] Ibid.

which choice is the right choice, and which side to fight on? Because no matter what you choose, you must stand for something. An example of this is Adam when he tells Neith:

> When you identified your life with the welfare of a group. You can go smashing through pain and death as easy as a pane of glass. You don't see them anymore than you see the glass: you see through and beyond. These men over in Russia who are leading the Revolution, they are like that. The Revolution to them is just glass: to be broken through. Into Freedom.[153]

Yet he has no real respect for the value of a woman other than what she can be to him. It becomes clearer how flawed Adam is in wanting a traditional wife when he and Neith are interacting with a female character described as a "philosophical anarchist" who defines marriage as a "bourgeois contract."[154] This occurs while Neith is in the company of Adam in "the Village" (Greenwich Village).[155]

Neith reflects on how "in her attempt to rationalize the ground either for accepting or rejecting Adam, that all her thoughts about him ended. He was so much in her mind as a symbol of destiny and so little yet as a person, that she had not been touched to anxiety."[156] This directly translates to Austin's philosophy about marriage being an act of necessity for most women in order to prosper, while for men it is a search for fulfillment. The author took pride in her own journey toward marriage as "she hadn't taken the first man that asked her, nor the first time asking… She had been entirely frank as to her intention towards a writing career."[157] This clearly shows how her approach to developing and writing about strong female characters is one aspect that related her literary figures to Austin's own story.

In 1920, the Washington, DC newspaper *The Evening Star* described Adam with the broad approach that "a man in his broad social vision and intent may actually be a voice crying in the wilderness, but that he may, at the same time, in his personal relations with a woman, or women, be as big a bounder as ever walked."[158] The notion is that the character trait within such a man displays

---

[153] Ibid., 323.
[154] Ibid.
[155] Wilson, *New York and the First World War*, 19-25.
[156] Austin, *No. 26 Jayne Street*, 169.
[157] Austin, *Earth Horizon*, 220.
[158] "No. 26 Jayne Street," *The Evening Star*, July 4, 1920, 19.

endless inconsistency, and the only vision of him is argued to be "inheritance, tradition, the long complacence of the world, [which] have blinded him to the righteousness of social fair-dealing when it comes to his own personal desires and vanities."[159]

Neith, much like Austin and the progressive-thinking women of the time, wants a union based on democracy, respect, *and* love, which is not something she will get from Adam; these ideas can be linked to later statements Austin makes in newspapers about how marriage in the form of balanced partnership is of great importance. In order to support this development, the story has several strong females who have diverted from the ideal of marriage and a domestic life, such as Aunt Emmy, the old maiden. One can argue that, in many ways, this offers up the old idea that strong women with opinions do not have/want a sexuality because of the stereotype that one cannot be both a wife and independent. Looking at US history and women's role in the war as workers, the Social Democratic Women's Federation started organizing non-profit groups for the benefit of women long before the peak of the war and had helped women access party press and express independence way back in 1901.[160]

Additionally, Austin breaks many stereotypes with the statement, "You see, I thought marriage was something that just happened to everybody. I never dreamed it wouldn't happen to me," and she goes on to write that "old maidens aren't different from other women. They want – everything."[161] The story calls on both Neith and the reader not to accept society's traditions easily, the argument being that such a mentality interferes with the new "self-Americanization."[162] Rose Matlock is, in many ways, what Neith is perhaps subconsciously striving to become, someone who claims that "the measure of war has been taken too long by women in terms of giving and grieving."[163] She also says that women will "never get it out of the prance and flourish class of experience until we apply to it the measure of other experiences."[164]

The final message to take away from Austin's story is that women are capable of making change all on their own, even without romanticized revolutionaries such as Adam Frear, or any other man, by their side: "[W]e've lived in a fool's paradise, we women … in a stage paradise of 'made love,'

---

[159] Ibid.
[160] Adickes, *To Be Young Was Very Heaven*, 107.
[161] Austin, *No. 26 Jayne Street*, 332.
[162] Ibid., 109.
[163] Ibid., 173.
[164] Ibid.

'influenced' idealism, 'cultivated' culture. We've played upon men. We've played at civilization. Now and then comes something like this war and upsets the play. I, for one, will play no more. I will not play!"[165] Eventually, Neith reaches the climactic point of radicalism, parallel with the war being at its most crucial point in Europe, saying, "I'm a suffragist now."[166] This character's progression and development can be linked back to the start of the novel when she was new to the social revolution and also hesitant to join the suffragette movement, as it had been described to her as "the keepsake habit of women that keeps them in bondage."[167]

Ultimately, the story portrays general principles through its characters; for example, Adam and Eustace are two opposite ideas, not just regular people. Through interactions with the two men, both the reader and Neith are made to face internal struggles: either to obey the principle or to challenge it – and face criticism. Ultimately what the story is about is political and social acceptance or revolution, albeit while being presented as a love story. The book was recognized, upon its publication, as having captured the emotional and intellectual events of Greenwich Village at war.[168]

The Rock Island Argus printed a review of *No. 26 Jayne Street* under the rubric "Books and Things" in July of 1920 and noted the work as being inspired by British literary individuals; this cross-comparison had not previously been made in any other newspaper. The novel is described as "handling viral issues of today, will bear comparison with the work of H.G. Wells and the best of the younger British novelists."[169] This makes the impact of Austin's time in and acquaintances from England a driving force of the novel. This perspective is not unlikely, as *No. 26 Jayne Street* draws upon the homecoming of an individual (the protagonist, Neith) who had been influenced by European culture for a long time, similarly to Austin herself.

Much like *The Young Woman Citizen*, *No. 26 Jayne Street* also faced financial difficulties upon its publication, which Austin addresses in *Earth Horizon* as leading her to temporarily abandon the common novel form.[170] She believed that it was her best work to date, however it was not popular because of its focus on personal radicalism, which contradicted the 'sleazy' mainstream

---

[165] Ibid., 315.
[166] Ibid., 264.
[167] Ibid., 74.
[168] Ibid.
[169] "Books and Things," *The Rock Island Argus* (Chicago, IL), July 24, 1920, 5.
[170] Austin, *Earth Horizon*, 337.

political expression.[171] The complex way in which Mary Hunter Austin thought was hard to process for the mainstream of the time; she believed that not even her publisher understood the points she was making because her points were ten to fifteen years ahead of their time.[172]

To sum up, the works read in this chapter are of two different kinds; there are the three main works that were introduced first, which were written at the exact time of the war, as well as 'contrasting' works outside of the timeline which conveyed messages of feminism, work, equal marriage, etc. that show that Austin was indeed feminist in her work because the war impacted her fiction as much as it impacted her as an individual.

Although many may not see some works, e.g. *The Ford*, as being of a notably feminist origin, the intent of introducing such works here was to look at the essence of her writing in parallel with the war rather than to draw something out of them that is not there. The works are not a feminist manifesto, but the ideas that are portrayed therein are clearly rooted in a feminist writer's mind. On the other hand, we have fictional works such as *No. 26 Jayne Street* which provide both fiction and feminism, however this comes with the luxury of being written after the war; the same goes for *Earth Horizon*. It is the political essays that have attracted second-wave feminist readers, however there is obviously more to unpack from her writing that goes unnoticed because they are not directly feminist in nature. Every single piece of writing penned during the war was transformative for Austin as a writer as well as both a feminist and a woman.

---

[171] Ibid.
[172] Ibid.

Chapter 4
Later Perceptions of Austin's Works

According to social and cultural historian Joyce Antler, feminism is a word that has obtained many different meanings since its introduction into our general vocabulary in the early 19th century.[1] Antler tries to define feminism and discuss its different appearances through time in a chapter published in 1994 in the edited collection *Feminist Struggles for Sex Equality: The History of Women in the United States*. The general idea is that feminism and gender equality have gone through many stages, often also interfering, both positively and negatively, with ideologies and class differences of different times.[2] Alternatively, as Ginette Castro wrote in 1990, "Feminism is the refusal to define all women and therefore all human beings solely in terms of sex."[3]

Feminist Struggles, edited by Nancy F. Cott, presents a beautiful collection of feminist, radical women and includes the chapter "Charlotte Perkins Gilman: A Feminist's Struggle with Womanhood" by Mary A. Hill. The chapter describes Gilman's radicalism as "rooted in an early struggle for independence, self-assertion, and self-respect,"[4] which essentially can be directly linked to all of the proto-feminists of the time (Austin included). Thus, the Women's Trade Union League became a helpful place for class-conscious women and early feminists, and it was through such unions that early feminist ideas blossomed.[5] Feminism in Austin's time can directly be described as radical practicality.

Through historical research, we can come closer to understanding whether the memory of the past, particularly in regard to Mary Hunter Austin's works, is correctly interpreted by 20th-century feminist scholars or whether the feminist interpretation of her literature is a modern construction. Being

---

[1] Joyce Antler, "Feminism as Life-Process: The Life and Career of Lucy Sprague Mitchell," in *Feminist Struggles for Sex Equality: The History of Women in the United States*, vol. 20, ed. Nancy F. Cott (Munich: Saur, 1994), 196-197.
[2] Ibid.
[3] Castro, *American Feminism*, 2.
[4] Mary A. Hill, "Charlotte Perkins Gilman: A Feminist Struggle With Womanhood," in *Feminist Struggles for Sex Equality: The History of Women in the United States*, vol. 20, ed. Nancy F. Cott (Munich: Saur, 1994), 142.
[5] Ibid., 166.

referenced by Progressive Women Conservationists as a feminist, as well as feminist in discussions of citizenship, Austin often wrote about differences between men and women. Gender was evidently one of the main hindrances of equality in her life. Consequently, her discussions about the difference of the "self" between men and women have been interpreted as feminist, according to the modern understanding of the term. The concept and construction of gender are discussed by Stacy Alaimo in "The undomesticated nature of feminism: Mary Austin and the progressive women conservationists."[6] Here, Alaimo takes a look at affect in American fiction, and the work from 1988 draws close to the aftermath of the second wave of feminists, who discuss ideas of gender construction. Alaimo deliberates on the idea that Austin takes normal "womanhood," which is commonly associated with femininity (meaning gender), and turns it against itself because women get exploited based on their gender. The fact is that Austin takes the traditionally set idea of feminine (wild) nature and turns it into something else, which results in a challenge to and pinpointing of the construction of gender and how it can be turned into anything – even an idea that the forces of nature and the biological female sex are able to resist.

However, Cott's historical look at how feminism has been understood in past eras in American women's history defines the understanding of 'feminism' in the 1910s and 1920s as something that has presented problems for historians because feminism has been used in such various manners. In the most literal sense, the women's suffrage movement's rebelliousness and the word 'feminism' were used to describe women's heightened expectations, expanded protests against male dominance, and efforts to redefine the hierarchy of gender.[7] Cott describes the claim to feminism as "a consciously modern claim: the women who so defined themselves saw their interests as breaking away from the established 'woman movement' of the nineteenth century."[8]

Cott captures a paradox in women's status, which claims "two seemingly contradictory visions of women's relation to society: the ideology of domesticity, which gave women a sex-specific role to play, primarily in the home; and feminism, which attempted to remove sex-specific limits on women's opportunities and capacities." The early definition of feminism,

---

[6] Alaimo, "The Undomesticated Nature of Feminism," 73-96.
[7] Nancy F. Cott, ed., *Feminist Struggles for Sex Equality: The History of Women in the United States*, vol. 20 (Munich: Saur, 1994), xi-xii.
[8] Ibid., xi.

according to Cott, was primarily driven by a change in women's own views of their domestic experience.[9]

Feminist Commemorations of Austin

Simply put, feminism, much like other 'isms,' is based on following a distinctive belief and interpretation of society, being or becoming almost like a philosophy or ideology for some people, in this case, the belief of equal rights regardless of biological sex or social gender.[10] However, how does one truly understand what feminism means across cultures and borders as well as time? In order to apprehend American feminism fully, both in the time of Austin and the time of those who analyzed her works, an approach, according to Karen Offen, is needed that includes the historical development of feminism to gain a better perspective.[11]

Offen goes into the distortionary definition that feminism is (in a complex combination) "a theory and/or movement concerned with advancing the position of women through such means as achievement of political, legal, or economic rights equal to those granted men."[12] It is obtaining the 'equal' part that is the truly fundamental ground of the concept and the movement, regardless of the time and place, for example at the 'birth' of the idea of feminism in 1848 at Seneca Falls concerning voting rights for women.[13] The aim of feminism was the notion of ending the inequality which served the advancement of men and did not extend to women, meaning unjust divisions of rights solely based on sex or gender. The celebration of differences is something that has also been historically significant since American suffragettes, labeled feminists in modern interpretations, were often content with the functions of their gender, despite the fight for equal political grounds. As an example, the statement that "Austin's concept of womanhood situates her within the discourse of cultural feminism"[14] is entirely biased because 'cultural feminism' and 'political activism' can be two distinct things that need to be evaluated as such. Austin agreed with her feminist 19th-century precursors and contemporaries that women are "maternal, cooperative,

---

[9] Ibid., 3.
[10] I am aware that there are diverse forms of feminism but, for reasons of space, this book only examines a few perspectives within the movement and definitions thereof.
[11] Karen Offen, "Defining Feminism: A Comparative Historical Approach," *Signs* 14, no. 1 (1988): 119-120.
[12] Ibid.
[13] Ibid.
[14] Schaefer, *Mary Austin's Regionalism*, 113.

altruistic, and life-affirmative."[15] Once again, the definition of feminism in the modern sense (i.e. sex equality) creates weakness because being maternal is seen as a disadvantage.

The term 'feminism' itself is a modern component of historical actions because the common usage of the term is more modern (20th century), which is why historical actions cannot always be aligned/justified with feminism as we know it.[16] Historically, many revolutionary movements assumed that questions of women's problems would be solved with a transition to socialism and more female involvement in production and/or the public sphere.[17] This is something we also witness in the case of Austin, as she publicly spoke about and openly demanded women's rights several times during the war years in the prime of her activism. Feminism cannot be defined entirely as one set of rules, as it varies from one century to another, and despite the fundamental aspects being attached to sex and gender, the overall intentions of individuals and movements (those for equality in the first wave and those for liberation in the second wave) fluctuate. Previously, the feminist tradition foresaw an egalitarian vision for social organization which would lead to equality of the genders, regardless of sex.[18]

In the 1960s, when the second wave of feminism rose to prominence, it was still not called feminism, but rather women's liberation, demanding equality in terms of pay, opportunity, sexual liberation with regard to abortion, divorce, and the basic needs of the female sex in their independent existence. It was an inclusive liberation for women all over the world, for workers in factories, and for student rights related to what the feminists at the time viewed as imperialistic university life. Much of the motivation rose from anger as women became more aware of their lack of privilege because of prejudice from society as well as official forces, for example, being paid 25% less for doing the same work as men, as well as being denied entry to workplaces based on their gender.[19] Abortions were illegal, and women were still the second sex despite their fights for voting and political rights all those years previously. The second feminist wave went even further as it created a

---

[15] Ibid.
[16] Offen, "Defining Feminism," 119-120.
[17] Michelle Friedman, Jo Metelerkamp and Ros Posel, "What Is Feminism? And What Kind of Feminist Am I?" *Agenda: Empowering Women for Gender Equity* 1 (1987): 20.
[18] Offen, "Defining Feminism," 135-136.
[19] Barbara Caine and Anne Summers, "Suffragettes to Social Media: Waves of Feminism." Lecture given at Sydney Opera House, Sydney, March 4, 2018.

consciousness and reinvented what it meant to be a woman.[20] Their purpose was to reform this specific meaning, as well as the world around them, demanding changes in laws regarding abortions, sexual assault, divorce, equal pay, contraceptives, public space, inclusivity in the job market, and general anti-discrimination laws.[21]

This point in particular creates a paradox between what Austin's actions stood for and what the new wave tried to achieve; where the author was attempting to own motherhood and femininity through streamlining women's skills, the new feminists wanted to turn away from these limitations to their sex. Feminists, much like other activists, had different approaches, such as individual feminism – which is perhaps the description most suited to Mary Austin's case. The individual feminist tradition is an approach that "emphasized more abstract concepts of individual human rights and celebrated the quest for personal independence (or autonomy) in all aspects of life."[22] However, this meant that they also downplayed and minimized the discussion linked to biological sex qualities, such as childbearing and all attendant responsibilities in relation to men,[23] which would be more important for the modern wave.

One of the important factors to include in feminist history and understanding is that it incorporates both a political and intellectual history of development. The history of feminism, both theoretically and politically, has developed into questions about nationalism, capitalism, and war and peace, parallel to the gender and equality questions of the time.[24] In the prime of Mary Austin's writing and activism during the war years, women's groups also experienced opposing developments, particularly because of the conflict between the relational and individualist perspectives. In the US, "individualist feminism gained momentum as increasing numbers of highly educated, single women intent on achieving personal autonomy became visible for the first time, [and] the participation of married women in the industrial labor force became a political issue...."[25] This is crucial to understanding why Mary Austin's interpreters gave her such significance in later years. She fitted a profile that served the 1960s concept of women's liberation and was from a movement of

---

[20] Offen, "Defining Feminism," 135-136.
[21] Ibid.
[22] Ibid.
[23] Ibid., 136.
[24] Ibid., 142.
[25] Ibid., 143.

women "born at a time of social upheaval in the capitalist world," a reaction rooted in both criticism and optimism.[26]

This development was the effect of capitalism on women and their role in the labor force after the Second World War when they were encouraged to go back to their motherly duties after their work efforts during the conflict.[27] The different kinds of feminism that developed in the 1960s and 1970s reflected a variety of social and class positions, and the women who came to bring forth their feminist beliefs also intertwined them with the different influences from their lives.[28] It is not unknown that women being excluded from debates in history was the norm before, however resistance has always been present, and the feminist scholar Valerie Bryson refers to this phenomenon as "feminist consciousness,"[29] which, using written sources, she traces as far back as 7th century Europe.[30] In the developing stages of the modern feminist movement during the 1960s, "some feminists have demanded to be included in 'malestream' ideologies, [and] many have also long argued that women are in important respects both different from and superior to men, and that the problem they face is not discrimination or capitalism but male power ... these ideas were developed into what came to be known as 'radical feminism.'"[31] The interesting aspect to take away from this is the development of what was viewed as radical before and after the First World War; Austin was a radical in her own time, but perhaps not so much by modern radical standards (naturally, this is generational). It is also important to note that Bryson's description of fighting the patriarchy, despite being similar to that of women in Austin's time in that it was motivated by political activity, economy, etc., had different origins and motives (e.g. the First World War and fundamental rights).

The earlier women's rights movements fought for equal political rights, influenced by different political ideas, while the modern ones branched out these pre-existing ideas (based on something else) into concrete feminist interpretations to try and reach an ideal society. In consequence, different feminisms existed: liberal feminism, socialist feminism, Marxist feminism, etc. The difference here is in how the practical ideology, or the other ideology, was based on the level of 'utopianism' in the root of the various 'isms.' These

---

[26] Friedman, Metelerkamp and Posel, "What is Feminism," 3-4.
[27] Ibid.
[28] Ibid., 4.
[29] Valerie Bryson, *Feminist Political Theory: An Introduction* (New York: Palgrave Macmillan, 2003), 5.
[30] Ibid.
[31] Ibid., 3.

may be small distinctions, such as "Marxism as a theory of social life is relatively unconcerned with sex,"[32] perhaps creating a paradox with the fundamental basis of feminism itself, which concerns itself with gender issues. Despite socialism having its roots in Marxism, there are small differences in the directions of feminist theories from claims such as this. Scholar and self-proclaimed socialist feminist Sally Alexander asks: "How can women speak and think creatively within Marxism when they can neither enter the narrative flow as fully as they wish, nor imagine that there might be subjectivities present in history [other] than those of class?"[33] She is emphasizing the difference that is portrayed here. The development of feminist thought has evidently been rooted in theoretical and practical disagreement, thus pinpointing all theories becomes close to impossible; however, the most relevant ones in this case (e.g. socialist feminism) will be discussed.[34] Despite Friedman's definitions of 'Marxist feminism,' socialist feminism is only based on Marx's writing, as Marx did not really have a feminist agenda. There was Marxism, then there was socialism, and then there was socialist feminism relating to Marx.

Thus, it is not incorrect to claim that there is no grand Marxist feminism, although there might be Marxists who are feminists, i.e. a Marxist feminist or a feminist Marxist, hence Marxist feminism has been described as "utopian."[35] This can be seen as a conflict of interest related to feminist interpretations. For example, liberal feminism was mostly promoted by middle-class women for their benefit, while Marxist and socialist feminism received the support of working-class (as well as middle-class) women.[36] This can be linked back to the women's rights movement consisting of suffragettes and those who supported women's rights, but not according to the socialist feminist interpretation. Modern liberal feminism argues that women's freedom should be based on the ability for women to choose their own lives and compete with men on equal terms in both the political and professional spheres. It is, therefore, on the grounds of equality that they are not against a capitalist system.[37] Wanting equal opportunities to succeed or fail on their

---

[32] Friedman, Metelerkamp and Posel, "What is Feminism," 13.
[33] Sally Alexander, "Women, Class and Sexual Differences in the 1830s and 1840s: Some Reflections on the Writing of a Feminist History," *History Workshop*, no. 17 (1984): 128.
[34] For a clear overview and a deep understanding of theories and directions within feminist political theories, Valerie Bryson's *Feminist Political Theory* serves as a spectacular academic insight.
[35] Friedman, Metelerkamp and Posel, "What is Feminism," 14.
[36] Ibid., 4.
[37] Ibid., 5-6.

own terms, liberal feminists also did not see the sex differences as problematic but rather as something to be celebrated (such as women's femininity).[38] This aspect of the feminist spectrum, which can also be seen at the time of the suffrage movement, is relational feminism, which is the idea focused on women's rights in interaction/relation to men, meaning the sexes strengthen each other's differences instead of negatively focusing on differentiation. Female contributions, such as the motherly and nurturing aspects, were positively claimed by the wider society in the early 1900s.[39] Additionally, the motherly trait resulted in the resourcefulness of women and the agency of Austin and like-minded women broadening at the time.

Liberal feminism in the 1960s and 1970s also argued that it would be beneficial for men, as it would no longer be solely their responsibility to elevate society and their families.[40] This is very similar to ideas Austin promoted in the 1910s with the encouragement of work for women in times of war, as she said that "this war calls for qualities in [a] woman which transcend her sex and establish her social value on her power to do, rather than on her power to give."[41] This means that it did not matter that women were not fighting actual battles because what they could offer was just as useful. Austin's investment in improvement came with skepticism as well, for instance in her role on a committee fighting unions that supported the committee for prohibition. Her view compared the behavior of the union leaders to that of a tyrannical state. The narrative in papers conveyed a message of enragement and reported on the dispute between the chambers of commerce in San Francisco and her efforts as a writer.[42]

Despite Austin being radical by her own time's standards,[43] modern radical feminism has gone much further than the liberal feminists and sought out the root of female oppression; thus, its main focus was to emphasize the patriarchy of the social system's hierarchical and dominating functions. They saw society as not only dominated by men but also shaped by and operating for male values, such as with regard to the economy and so on.[44] Radical

---

[38] Ibid., 5-7.
[39] Ibid.
[40] Ibid., 7.
[41] Ibid.
[42] "Il Congresso Degli Scrittori e Dei Giornalisti," *L'Italia* (San Francisco), May 24, 1915, 4.
[43] "Feminists were more rebellious than conventionally respectable suffragists and socialists, who clung to the ideal of womanly virtue." Adickes, *To Be Young Was Very Heaven*, 89.
[44] Friedman, Metelerkamp and Posel, "What is Feminism," 8-16.

feminists in America saw personal issues (social, sexual, etc.) as political ones, such as the male to female relationship and its dynamics.[45] In regard to Marxist feminism, Marxism as a theory does not concern itself with sex but rather with workers (regardless of gender). Classical Marxism did not alarm itself with the oppression of women in the workplace, and "[b]ecause of their primary responsibility for the household and childcare, women were condemned to seclusion in the home. This exclusion from public life and particularly the workplace meant that they were excluded from participating in collective action to change their own lives as members of the working class."[46] This was despite the feminist perspective being that once class problems were fixed, gender imbalance would be as well.[47] Karl Marx's (1818-1883) friend, the German philosopher Friedrich Engels (1820-1895), took a more detailed approach to the concepts of unpaid work and women serving under their husbands in the home in unacknowledged work. Engels can be seen as the basis for modern arguments and research in the field; for example, there are echoes of him in the modern discussion about equal wages for women because, ultimately, women served 'under' men if they were not making money themselves.[48]

Classical Marxist feminism thus served as the most efficient form, despite being gender-blind, much like the socialists of Austin's time who were both color- and gender-blind, despite not pushing colored or women's issues in reality. Considering socialism's inclusion, the question of women was later put more into the light by August Bebel (1840-1913), who analyzed women's oppression under capitalism in *Women and Socialism*.[49] It was Bebel who expressed an increased socialist interest in feminism, and the scholars Michelle Friedman, Jo Metelerkamp, and Ros Posel write that socialist feminism included the domestic aspects that Marxist feminism ignored. They also describe socialist feminism as an optimistic political tendency because, theoretically, it contains the potential for change as it rejects any biologically determined sexual division of the workforce and states the ideology's feminist philosophy,[50] claiming that the differences between women and men are not pregiven but something socially constructed, thus making them also socially alterable.[51] We can link this to Judith Butler's *Gender Trouble* and further

---

[45] Ibid.
[46] Ibid., 13.
[47] Ibid.
[48] Ibid.
[49] August Bebel, *Woman and Socialism* (New York: Socialist Literature Company, 1910).
[50] Friedman, Metelerkamp and Posel, "What is Feminism," 11-13.
[51] Ibid., 16.

studies that argue that gender is a social construction, i.e. 'gender performativity,' that it changes with time, race, social class, and geography, and that it is difficult to separate culture from its development.[52]

In the modern approach to capitalism and gender (ultimately, two of the most important components of modern feminism), it has become clear that one cannot make generalizations because of the importance of context, e.g. capitalistic systems creating greater inequality between the sexes; in order to analyze such developments, one must analyze development within this context to reach a conclusion. Thus, the approach that developed was to include both gender and social class.[53] In the 1980s, Lourdes Beneria and Gita Sen were among those who advanced this analytical approach to determine what factors to include in gender-related approaches. They focused on both gender and class as factors, and as the approach became wider over the years, it started to include race, ethnicity, and other hallmarks of identity such as sexuality.[54] This methodology can be interpreted as the modern development of the analysis that is impacting our understanding of Austin's time in a more fundamental/biased way than we are aware of because it involves modern perceptional norms.

Where liberal feminism sought out individual freedom, socialist feminists wanted shared social achievement, which in many ways is similar to Marxism, but the difference is that socialists wanted freedom in the home as well as in the public domain.[55] In modern feminism, women 'group' together to fight the 'patriarchy,' and thus, despite their directions varying, their common goal is to end male exploitation. Feminism, through its development, became part of the fundamental aspect of intellectuality and politics in society, and in order to locate its historical evolution and the differences in the ideologies, one must study the shift within the movement. Despite said shifts, it is important to note that the fundamental drive based on collective sex struggles has stayed the same. In modern developed societies, the aim is to succeed in forming a world without gender bias.

---

[52] Judith Butler, *Gender Trouble*, (New York, London: Routledge, 2006), 6-7. For further reading on gender (identity, performativity, etc.) and feminism, see Halina Filipowicz, "'Am I That Name?' Feminism, Feminist Criticism, and Gender Studies," *The Polish Review* 59, no. 1 (2014): 3-15.
[53] Lourdes Beneria, Günseli Berik and Maria S. Floro, *Género, Desarrollo y Globalización: Una Visión desde la economía feminista* (Barcelona: Routledge, 2018), 40-41.
[54] Ibid. For further reading, see Lourdes Beneria, "Conceptualizing the Labor Force: The Underestimation of Women's Economic Activities," *The Journal of Development Studies* 17, no. 3 (1981): 10-28.
[55] Friedman, Metelerkamp and Posel, "What is Feminism," 16.

In order to understand the shifts mentioned above, one must study memory vs. history. The memory of the past is a reconstruction; thus, it is what is remembered – and not necessarily (in great detail) the tale of the time. The way Austin has been read since the 1960s and 1970s within the feminist movement is entirely the voice of that specific era and is perhaps not quite so related to the original message written by the author herself in the earlier years of the 1900s. To name just one example, the feminist English professor Elaine Showalter follows the narrative,[56] which is why she addresses Austin's works as an "important contribution to the 1920s feminist theory"[57] and claims her to be a "fighting feminist."[58] Showalter draws on the narrative that Austin's influence came from the empowerment of her mother, despite the two not having a close relationship. The impact of the writer's relationship with her mother as a source of inspiration while she was growing up is also debated by Elizabeth Wright, who claims that the writer and her mother "shared interest in feminist issues."[59] What a feminist is in today's modern society, what it was in the 1960s and 1970s, and what it was in Mary Hunter Austin's time have completely different answers: they are not similar, and thus we must pinpoint the reason why they have been interpreted or considered to be similar, looking to the aspect of historical memory. One of the most accurate descriptions of the discrepancy between Austin's time and the confident parallel of feminist claims in the 1960s and 1970s is offered by Showalter: "Feminists of the 1920s often saw their problems as the inevitable turmoil of transition,"[60] ultimately clarifying the argument that the concept of feminism was not the one of Austin's time because the movement is, and has always been, a developing process. Another feminist referring to Austin is Professor Arlyn Diamond, who was one of the founding figures of the Program in Women's Studies at the University of Massachusetts.[61] Diamond and Lee R. Edwards describe Austin as exotic, highlighting that she was "involved in radical political movements of her time" and was also "an active supporter of the cause of feminism, birth control, and socialism."[62]

---

[56] New York State Writers Institute, "Elaine Showalter," accessed May 5, 2019, https://www.albany.edu/writers-inst/webpages4/archives/showalter_elaine09.html.
[57] Elaine Showalter, *These Modern Women: Autobiographical Essays from the Twenties* (New York: The Feminist Press, 1989), 79.
[58] Ibid., 3.
[59] Ibid., 78-79; Wright, "Mary Hunter Austin," 13.
[60] Wright, "Mary Hunter Austin," 14.
[61] UMass Amherst Libraries, "Arlyn, Diamond, 1941-," accessed May 5, 2019, http://scua.library.umass.edu/umarmot/diamond-arlyn-1941/.
[62] Lee R. Edwards and Arlyn Diamond, *American Voices, American Women* (New York: Avon, 1973), 255.

Diamond's analysis of the exotic is true to who Austin was, because it is clear that Mary Austin was an exotically perceived individual even in New York, where she was surrounded by intellectuals who alleviated perceptions of her. However, to a certain degree, she remained alien due to her Californian past and her involvement with the Native American population, as well as her travels in Europe. In New York, the author was described as flourishing into society and portrayed as having moved to benefit both herself and New York: "She did not remain on the edge of the desert.... Now she lives in a house facing on Gramercy Park, New York, where she has a studio. She has exchanged the Mojave Desert for the desert of Manhattan, but she is sheltered in an oasis touched with the lingering loveliness of New York."[63] One can surmise that the value of the writer was in her empiric value, in the context of her new setting. American liberals evidently maintained the value of New York City: "If you haven't seen the Grand Canyon you had better keep away from the Liberal Club; but once you have caught the lift and bigness of America outside New York, then New York is the most inspiring place in the world in which to work."[64] The message of this article was supposed to be applied to Austin's case, of course. The novelist is portrayed as a token of the exotic wilderness who was tamed in New York in order to serve a purpose of the greater intellectual good.

Maurice Halbwachs (1877-1945) claims that "it is in society that people normally acquire their memories. It is also in society that they recall, recognize, and localize their memories,"[65] thus explaining that using collective recollection to build a feminist identity means that shared experience gets many voices, and is not the agency of a single agenda, or a history in the traditional sense. German scholar Jan Assmann argues, in agreement with Halbwachs, that memory is not history.[66] The applicable factor here is the collective belief of feminists' perceptions of Austin. History works in a reverse manner to collective memory: where collective memory only focuses on similarities and continuity, history provides nothing but differences and discontinuity. Collective memory looks at a certain group from the inside, while history leaves out any period without change as an empty interlude in the story so that the only worthwhile historical facts are those that include real events or processes resulting in something new. Group memory, thus, lays emphasis on its distinction from all other group memories, i.e. its uniqueness, and history eliminates all such differences and

---

[63] "Books and the Book World," *The Sun*, October 13, 1918, 6.
[64] Ibid.
[65] Halbwachs, *On Collective Memory*, 38.
[66] Assmann, *Cultural Memory*, 28.

recognizes facts within a homogenous historical context in which nothing is unique, everything is comparable to everything else, each individual episode is linked to other episodes, and they are all of equal significance.[67] The writing of feminism becomes a concept of its own, and 'her-story' develops into an agenda. The concept of feminist writing is deemed as nothing by historians and is, in modern fields, considered more as 'social history' if anything, and is therefore often more analytical than a constructive narrative.[68] This is the exact argument where one can point to the modern interpretations of Austin because, historically, her books and efforts have been 'left out' in favor of political events of the First World War, while modern feminist interpretations have gone back to them and applied strength through collective memory and supplementary tradition. Re-evaluations have applied significance to every single action, both personal and literary, and this is more or less what happens when we go back and read every mention of her in the news: we give Mary Hunter Austin new importance by looking at every single detail of her life unfold; historically, she was much more low key in the war years because, previously, the focal point was elsewhere. An example of this is *The Young Woman Citizen* going unnoticed in favor of more important social issues. Halbwachs writes that creating a collective memory also means pushing aside parts of what does not fit into the constructed memory (the shared history), which is the modern turn re-readings took, and he explains it by dividing memory into two groups, one made from habits and turned toward action, and another which involves a certain disinterest in present life.[69]

In history, prior to the establishment of a collective understanding of gender difference, remembering constituted seeing a collective identity in a process.[70] In the 1960s and 1970s, post-colonial feminists were trying to recreate that remembrance according to the modern feminist tradition and establish agency by their reliance on Austin and her works. The author's early agency helped create a sense of collective unity and continuity (and identity) within the tradition of feminism, and ultimately collective identity through the development of memory-anchoring through modifications.[71] This is possible through the unavailability of the original experience and the limited fragmentary and intervened nature of the reconstruction.[72] Halbwachs refers

---

[67] Ibid., 29.
[68] Gro Hagemann, *Feminisme Og Historieskriving* (Oslo: Universitetsforlaget, 2001), 29-31.
[69] Halbwachs, *On Collective Memory*, 47.
[70] Marianne Hirsch and Valerie Smith, "Feminism and Cultural Memory: An Introduction," *Signs* 28, no. 1 (2002): 4.
[71] Halbwachs, *On Collective Memory*, 41-42.
[72] Ibid., 46.

to this as "[s]ocial classes and their tradition" and goes on to discuss how, in every era, projects, movements, and suchlike can be accomplished better than previously. The reason for this is that earlier societies might not have seen the need for the accomplishment of the projects and movements in question; however, moving forward and being absorbed with something else can result in going back and refocusing.[73] In this case, the new focus was on feminism, thus going back and refocusing was on the first big collective women's rights movement to serve the second. The social frameworks of memory function through influence and essential human matters.[74] Assmann's idea is that accounts of origins, groups, or personal matters are processed in different stages, and in modern times, because of the abundance of information, we can 'travel' back and forth through this information.[75]

The creation of a feminist identity was a process heavily based on memory, which Assmann describes as the faculty that enables us to form an awareness of selfhood (identity), both on the personal and the collective level.[76] The scholar debates that identity, in this case a feminist identity, in its turn is related to time. A human self is a 'diachronic identity,' built "of the stuff of time,"[77] which is exactly how the new feminist reading of Austin's literature was potentially handled; it developed a new 'self' and modern meaning over time.

Personal memory is described as a matter of one's neurocentral system; it is personal and individual, and this was the only recognized memory until the late 1920s. Cultural memory, which is the type of memory under discussion here, is more collective than personal: "Whereas knowledge has a universalist perspective, a tendency toward generalization and standardization, memory, even cultural memory, is local, egocentric, and specific to a group and its values."[78] Going back and re-reading Austin's literature, and making it impactful, is creating tradition from an idea more than a direct truth. This creation of tradition from memory is as problematic as it is difficult because it is

---

[73] Ibid., 120-122.
[74] Ibid., 162.
[75] Assmann, *Cultural Memory*, 34.
[76] Jan Assmann, "Communicative and Cultural Memory," in *Cultural Memory Studies: An International and Interdisciplinary Handbook*, eds. Astrid Erll and Ansgar Nünning (Berlin: De Gruyter, 2008), 109-110.
[77] Ibid., 109. For further reading, see Thomas Luckmann, "Remarks on Personal Identity: Inner, Social and Historical Time," in *Identity: Personal and Socio-Cultural*, ed. Anita Jacobson-Widding (Atlantic Highlands, NJ: Humanities, 1983), 67-91.
[78] Assmann, "Communicative and Cultural Memory," 113.

hard to trace the invention of these traditions.[79] In this case, we know where the fundamental basis comes from – the author and the literature – however, the altering of the narrative to fit modern society (feminism) should be questioned.

During the second wave of feminism, female scholars started to want more inclusion for what they had to say, but they also wanted more women to be included in the grand picture of history. An example within universities is the rise and development of gender history as a field of research. Gender history, a valid part of the second wave, started examining how, for instance, we think about history itself, which is why in many ways the idea was similar to the history of mentalities, but not exactly the same. Some feminist scholars describe it as a compromise of knowledge about history, in that it is the product of a collection of scholars' concerns about the past.[80] The aspect of gender in history is based on the primary idea that what it means to be defined as a man or a woman has a history of its own.[81] While fighting for liberation, women also strengthened their sense of belonging in history: the gendered history of mentalities. One can therefore argue that the modern feminist perception about Austin can not only be linked to the development of the field of women's liberation but also to the development of gender history as a method, as it gave more grounds for events and individuals to serve modern readings and strengthen feminism within the humanities.[82] The rise and expansion of women's history contributed to a rethinking of history altogether, as with the history of mentalities.[83] The empowered women's movement of the late 1960s provided the substance for the field of women's history to emerge, and with this, the strength to re-write aspects of society.[84] Women had more or less been left out of historical writing, and thus the first attempts at reclaiming their historical place centered on combining the chronicles for appropriate figures to demonstrate that female notables of similar authority to males did indeed exist.[85] The creation of tradition and memory, as discussed by other important scholars, became particularly

---

[79] Eric Hobsbawm and Terence Ranger, *The Invention of Tradition* (Cambridge: Cambridge University Press, 2000), 4-5.
[80] Sonya O. Rose, *What Is Gender History?* (Malden, MA: Polity Press, 2010), 1.
[81] Ibid., 2. For further reading on gender in historical analysis, see Joan W. Scott, "Gender: A Useful category in Historical Analysis," *The American Historical Review* 91, no. 5 (1986): 1053-1075.
[82] Rose, *What Is Gender History*, 3.
[83] Ibid., 4.
[84] Linda L. Lindsey, *Gender Roles: A Sociological Perspective*, 5th ed. (Boston, MA: Pearson Education Inc., 2011), 102-103.
[85] Ibid.

exemplary. Mary Austin's agency, and stories, discussed individual identity to some extent, however these individuals were shaped by groups (socialist and women's rights ideas). However, the modern feminist narrative, by focusing on these singular stories of Austin's works, would better highlight that the individual and the public/social could come together:

> Cultural memory, they seem to suggest, can best be understood at the juncture where the individual and the social come together, where the person is called on to illustrate the social formation in its heterogeneity and complexity. The individual story, whether told through oral narrative, fiction, film, testimony, or performance, also serves as a challenge and a counter memory to official hegemonic history.[86]

The agency of Austin was not one and the same as the collective one of modern feminists; she was limited but fought the system, and it was on similar grounds to these that her philosophies have been re-read: modern readers' efforts intended to create an epistemology into which Austin would come and help to provide deeper roots for contemporary ideas. The distinguished existence of feminist nature is the common ground for the elaboration of a feminist epistemology. Women's history has been persistent since its beginning, rebellious in the struggle for "a history of our own," a "language of our own,"[87] and the fundamental right to determine female sexuality freely. Using the mixture of political and public history as a method to advance different goals and messages is not uncommon, and Norwegian historians Jan Bjarne Bøe and Ketil Knutsen have written about how political parties use history as a tool to take credit for fundamental welfare in society in order to gain more followers. This is a prime example of constructing the narrative and, thus, changing the memory.[88] What we can gather from this didactical approach is that post-colonial feminists, in all areas of society (universities, workplaces, domestic locales, etc.), had the common goal of forwarding the gender fight. Thus, they used a mixture of political and social history to re-define Austin.[89]

It was Austin who wished to exist outside of the system, which was not only the male-dominated system but also that of systematic female grouping,

---

[86] Hirsch and Smith, "Feminism and Cultural Memory," 7.
[87] Alexander, "Women, Class and Sexual Differences," 127.
[88] Jan Bjarne Bøe and Ketil Knutsen, *Innføring i Historiebruk* (Oslo: Cappelen Damm Høyskoleforlaget, 2013), 93-125.
[89] Ibid.

because the latter was too limiting for her ideas.[90] She describes the time in which she was involved in suffrage matters as important but also as a time in which she would be held back by others, who corrected her and standardized her to the point where she was bored with suffrage entirely, as the author recalls in *Earth Horizon*, although she wished to "keep the public on the beaten track."[91]

This idea of existing outside of the system is similar to post-colonial ideas presented by the feminist scholar Gayatri Chakravorty Spivak in Asunción Oliva Portolés' book *Miradas Feministas: Del Postcolonialismo A La Globalización*,[92] where the argument and idea are that it is impossible to perform at full capacity in an already-established system, particularly as a woman at that time (a second-class citizen in comparison to men); thus, changing the system is ultimately the only thing that will help.[93] Through attempting to make a political change, Austin was attempting to change the foundations, instead of just herself.

Her self-empowerment was different to that of the regular suffragettes because she pushed those boundaries in order to get the benefits she wanted, which feminists later wanted to push even further. Her capacity to exist independently was fueled by her socialistic political beliefs; social and political criticism is what drove her, more than her desire to break down sex-based barriers. The structure of the author's existence was not evidently dominated by any system, despite her dabbling in religion, marriage, and other potentially shackling structures; she explored but was not limited. Her radical ideas (for the time) inspired the collective agencies of a group. Foucault suggests that the function of the intellectual is to "[n]o longer to place himself 'somewhat ahead and to the side' in order to express the truth of the collectivity; rather, it is to struggle against the forms of power that transform him into its object and instrument in the sphere of 'knowledge,' 'truth,' 'consciousness' and 'discourse,'"[94] which is very evident in the change within the writer.

---

[90] Mary Austin, "Women as Pacifists," *New York Tribune*, February 17, 1917, 8.
[91] Austin, *Earth Horizon*, 327.
[92] Asunción Oliva Portolés, *Miradas Feministas: Del Postcolonialismo A La Globalización* (Madrid: Pulmen S.L.L., 2016), 42-43.
[93] Ibid. For further reading on post-colonial feminism and institutional criticism, see Gayatri Chakravorty Spivak, *The Post-Colonial Critic: Interviews, Strategies, Dialogues*, ed. Sara Harasym (New York: Chapman and Hall, 2014), 1-16.
[94] Michel Foucault, *Language, Counter-memory, Practice: Selected Essays and Interviews*, ed. Donald F. Bouchard (New York: Cornell University Press, 1980), 207-208.

Perhaps the reason Austin's expressions lived on was because of their openness to re-reading, as her literature was rooted in radical ideas that remain open to interpretation to this day. On a personal level, she continued to break free from social limitations, such as the shame society made her feel about having a disabled child: "Perhaps you know, because everybody seems to know it, that my little daughter was one of those who suffer for the sins of the fathers. But what everybody doesn't know is that she is still living in an institution in California, and [is] a secret source of care and pain to me."[95] Austin states this in a letter to Elizabeth Jordan, dated 5 April 1915. The letter's content also addresses one factor of Austin's motive that is not often discussed, which is her need for money. Modern interpretations often paint Austin as wholeheartedly artistic for the sake of selfless art, intellectuality, and as a voice of reason, but the true foundation is in her eclecticism. However, it is important to note that her intellectual imputes had many motives, among which was money as a driving force: "[S]omething has come up important to her future, which makes a demand of me for more money than I can at present lay my hands on."[96] And the letter ends with "please destroy this letter." This makes it clear that the unhappy mother felt ashamed of this side of her, more so about her need for money than her disabled daughter's condition. The issue of money is present because of the critical state of the economy due to American interference in the First World War and it is clear that Austin is eager to make a living, yet she does not sell her integrity short when she argues that too much impute from others will not be tolerated.[97] She discusses her concern about Miss Jordan's interference in her creative process and makes it clear that even though her financial situation is critical, her creativity cannot be pushed.[98]

Butler's well-known definition of gender can also be used to discuss Austin's case: "If gender is the cultural meanings that the sexed bodies assume, then a gender cannot be said to follow from a sex in any one way."[99] The question of whether gender is something that one is or something that one has is the basis from which Austin's 'proto-feminism' was translated to appeal to

---

[95] Mary Hunter Austin to Elizabeth Garver Jordan, New York, April 5, 1915, New York Public Library, Rare Books and Manuscripts, Elizabeth Garver Jordan Papers, Box 1, Folder 6, 1.
[96] Ibid.
[97] Mary Hunter Austin to Elizabeth Garver Jordan, New York, July 13, 1915, New York Public Library, Rare Books and Manuscripts, Elizabeth Garver Jordan Papers, Box 1, Folder 6, 1.
[98] Ibid.
[99] Butler, *Gender Trouble*, 6.

modern norms and new ideas. Feminist theories from the 1960s onward have claimed that gender is the cultural interpretation of sex: simply put, it is culturally constructed, and the question is whether this construction can be changed to sustain a more balanced society for equality purposes.[100] One can claim that modern interpretations, such as those of Butler in which "sex is not gender" and "gender is fluid," were not the direct intentions of Austin, as women in the earlier 1900s wanted empowerment as women, rather than to be empowered as anything else; however, she revolted, and she respected and envied female revolt as such.

Jan Assmann argues that strength and weakness in tradition come from the presence (or lack) of repetition,[101] and since the main component of feminism is sex but the outcome is different, one finds something of a gray area. In other words, while feminism is present in the subject matter (Austin's war-year literature), the type of feminism is different. Ellen Lewin's *Feminist Anthropology* (2009) discusses how the underlying task of feminism is the question of how to define and recognize the status of men and women, which is a balance/status that varies.[102] Based on some of the comparisons made in earlier chapters, it is clear that the impact of the First World War on the late writer was more politically-driven feminism than feminism for the sake of gender; her objectives were more toward ensuring democracy, and the question of interest is how women could contribute to this. Austin consequently valued women for what they could do in the fight rather than what they could not do because society claimed it was for men.

The main argument, and conclusion, of this study should not be whether Austin was feminist in nature or not because, as we have witnessed in newspapers and her writing, her intentions could be indeed called feminist, but to whom? To modern interpretations or to her own time? It is almost unfair to limit her efforts to the single word 'feminist,' as she was doing more than fighting for gender equality. Her literary works between 1914 and 1920 became culturally valuable pieces in her own time, but even more so after their later re-interpretation. References to Austin as "a radical feminist" were not something to be read in the papers too often until much later, and the term became more common in reference to her after the 1960s and 1970s, such as when she was called a "feminist alternative to the masculinist myths

---

[100] Ibid., 7.
[101] Assmann, *Cultural Memory*, 234-236.
[102] Ellen Lewin, *Feminist Anthropology: A Reader* (Hoboken, NJ: John Wiley & Sons, 2009), 18.

of the far West."[103] This can be enhanced by looking at contemporary sources without any modern bias, such as the article "Young Woman and Her Part in War" from 1918 published in the activist paper *The Knoxville Independent*.[104] The discussion that the author was presenting is more about making women a resource and more efficient than about a race of the sexes.[105] Austin's message was not directed at women who were housewives, nor those who were earning a wage, but at those who existed without purpose. The narrative was simply to take ownership of their citizenship in order to contribute by learning book-keeping, typewriting, or even electrical work if they lived in rural places where it would be highly needed, as well as to seek to pass civil service examinations. With headlines such as "Women Display Keen Interest in School of Voting," the news sources documented that *The Young Woman Citizen* was used as one of the books to teach this subject matter and that it was included on the list of books that are helpful to one's development (of understanding one's citizenship).[106] This is in many ways a display of what the post-war era had in store for Austin's work (especially *The Young Woman Citizen*), which gained no significant attention during the conflict period but gained perhaps a more appreciative audience in the years after.

The Young Woman Citizen gaining more political momentum after its intended time is paralleled by Austin herself, insofar as she gained more individual feminist value in the second wave of feminism than she did during the suffragette movement. Austin's encouragements to become a valuable citizen were political but also rather society-oriented, as she encouraged women to "find out the most valuable skill and save that for your country."[107] During the first wave of feminism, *The Young Woman Citizen* was used as one of the books to teach this subject matter and more, and how she gained more acknowledgment on (feminist) matters was rather overlooked when the book was first presented. Since the First World War played an important role in the development of the women's rights movement, this interrelationship should be examined more closely here.

This idea can be linked to the modern feminist fight for working-class women's rights and empowerment, but at the time, it was because of war and

---

[103] Rudnick, "Feminist on the Frontier," 22.
[104] Mary Austin, "Young Woman and Her Part in War," *The Knoxville Independent*, June 29, 1918, 7.
[105] Ibid.
[106] "Women Display Keen Interest in School of Voting," *The News Scimitar*, October 25, 1920, 5.
[107] Ibid.

not equality. The war offered more women the chance for waged work – be it on a farm, in factories, or office jobs, the number of opportunities grew within the US with the development of the war. Historian David M. Kennedy states that despite the continuous belief of this idea, the reality was that women's employment in the war was limited, and those who took heavily industrialized jobs to provide for their families had abandoned the positions by 1919.[108] The challenge was in returning to daily life and rebuilding the domestic life that had existed prior to the war when the foundations had already been shaken and the gender roles challenged during the conflict. Women had to vacate themselves from the waged workforce and resume their domestic duties, even if they did not wish to do so. The value of motherhood was once again used as agency, however from a different angle to before. Where motherhood was previously synonymous with strength, now being a mother was a domestic question.[109] This was also a problem in the family dynamic after the First World War. Aside from the efforts for more waged work, many also began their efforts for more complete citizenship rights, despite being touched less by the violence of the war.[110] Activists in the movement for women's suffrage were, however, divided over supporting the conflict. Neither the proactive protesters nor the moderates working in the factories can alone claim the achievement of getting the Nineteenth Amendment passed in 1920, which ensured equal voting rights and no prejudice based on sex. This particular triumph was a collective effort, effected by all women in different positions and with different motives: pacifists, literati, industrial workers, or otherwise.[111] This is the tone that one can detect in Austin's intentions in the press, and her work, during the years in question. An article in the democratic, and highly anti-corruption newspaper, *The Chicago Eagle*,[112] from May of 1918 gives an indication of what kind of newspapers invested in the writer's narrative and mentions her addressing the "sex emancipation of women as a result of the war" and discussing some of the psychological and emotional setbacks of the new era of women's independence, as it was not all positive.[113] The article does not go into any further detail other than that particular quote, yet it can be linked not only to

---

[108] Kennedy, *Over Here*, 285.
[109] Ibid., 119-120.
[110] Ibid., 284.
[111] Ibid.
[112] The newspaper's motto being "independent in all things, neutral in none" as well as "fearless and truthful."
[113] "The May Forum," *Chicago Eagle*, May 11, 1918, 4.

The Young Woman Citizen (which was published in 1918) but also to the efforts of women toward the finalization of the Nineteenth Amendment.[114]

Modern interpretations about this narrative of feminism are again more related to the question of cultural memory. This story of the women's movement fight became symbolic, the epiphany of patriotism relating to ideas of fluid gender instead of sex. The reason for this is that despite the use of the word 'feminism' by the modern women's movement, the first wave of the movement was about political equality, while the second was about the liberation of the female sex. The result was that the second wave developed a new language and culture, which they applied to the earlier movement. Halbwachs addresses this in *One Collective Memory* as a phenomenon of priority shifts in different eras.[115]

Further elaborating on the theme of 'interpretations,' one must highlight that Austin herself often drew parallels between England and the United States, interpreting their politics and explaining that England was more structured and efficient in the use of women's contributions and how to learn from this. She believed that the First World War was different for women because the way it was fought required more "typically female" skills than previous wars, where direct battles were men's playgrounds: "this war calls for qualities in woman which transcend her sex and establish her social value on her power to do, rather than on her power to give."[116] This means that it did not matter that women were not fighting actual battles, because what they could offer was just as useful as what men had to offer. Statements such as this are powerful and clear up why she could be called a feminist in the modern sense. The author was political; however, the constructing of the past offers her viewpoints a modern value that we seek and find in history. Jacques Le Goff's article "Mentalities: A History of Ambiguities" talks about the attraction of history lying in its vagueness and argues that it can be used to refer to "the left-overs," meaning that a historical analysis can be made of even the most "indefinable residues."[117]

Austin's fundamental ideas on war and women's ethical, political, and social roles continued to appear in newspapers after the war, when her political and social works gained more importance. *The News Scimitar* was one paper in which the growing political interest among women in 1920 was considered to be a direct result of the First World War, as well as the new emancipation of women.

---

[114] Adickes, *To Be Young Was Very Heaven*, 98-100.
[115] Halbwachs, *On Collective Memory*, 120.
[116] Ibid.
[117] Le Goff, "Mentalities," 166-176.

The first wave of feminism, to which one can assign Austin, was about the emancipation of women and women's rights and covered the period between the French Revolution and the First World War.[118] The roots of the movement can perhaps be best linked to the fact that upon the writing of many new declarations, women came to realize that they were not equal in these rights, which were solely based on sex. However, the feminist perspective at that specific time was highly encouraged by political discontent, perhaps more so than by direct sex emancipation. Austin was among the women who were in on creating a direct and effective anti-war strategy.[119] She was politically critical, more so than she was gender-driven at times, and although her ideas resonate with those of socialist feminism, these are often later feminist constructions and interpretations than actual notions of her time. This is important to remember, as it is a key element in later feminist reconstructions when creating a new narrative.

Historian Ross J. Wilson confirms that despite the lack of American involvement in the early years of the war, its authority was still ever so present where matters of identity and citizenship were concerned.[120] New York was not only the ideal place for the development of Mary Austin, it was also described as a haven for social and political objectors, revolutionaries, and radicals. The breakout of the war in Europe in 1914 created a new order, and residents were asked to demonstrate their allegiance to the United States across communities, a process which only intensified when the nation became involved in the conflict in 1917.[121] This goes to explain Austin's alarmed debates on the subject matter of the citizenship of women in her writing and activism: this was part of politics, not just culture and society. In February of 1917, two months before the United States joined the war, Austin expressed her thoughts in an article titled "Women as Pacifists" in *The New York Tribune*.[122] The subtitle read "Why Mrs. Mary Austin Feels Constrained to Resign from the Women's Peace Party – Feminism vs. Society as a Whole."[123] This was an escalation as a result of war tension. Before the war and the intensified global situation, one could claim the author's intentions of putting women's best interests forward to be socially radical (and dangerous to the patriarchy). However, because of the war, her ideas and beliefs were

---

[118] Caine and Summers, "Suffragettes to Social Media."
[119] Bennett, *Radical Pacifism*, 6.
[120] Wilson, *New York and the First World War*, 15.
[121] Ibid., 14-15.
[122] Mary Austin, "Women as Pacifists," *New York Tribune*, February 17, 1917, 8.
[123] Ibid.

celebrated and not dismissed as ludicrous. The war gave Austin a window to be a 'normal' person among radicals instead of a radical among normal people (which would be the case in a society unaffected by distress).

As previously mentioned, Austin maintained that women were against war because it threatened their subjective interests more than those of any other class in society. This debate primarily considers women as a social class, dependent on a hierarchy related to the female sex. This brings us to the concept of contradictions. The primary marvel underlying the history of the feminist movement of the 19th and early 20th century was the impact of industrialization on women. It contributed to creating different classes among women themselves, unfortunately.[124] The combination of cultural, political, and economic factors resulted in noteworthy differentiations between the situations of women and men in the industrial force, as well as among women themselves.[125]

One of the essential factors that later analysis can pin on the overall impact was the solid development and formation of a feminist alliance that went across class conflicts in the form of the New York Women's Trade Union League in the years between 1903 and 1914.[126] This is perhaps one of the things that were used as a motivator when the second wave of feminists came to re-write the history of sisterhood and claim more rights. However, this was a naïve belief. During the early period, feminists often based their intentions on two more or less contradictory grounds. First, women demanded the same political and legal rights, however they also wanted special treatment because of their physiological differences, e.g. the biological ability to give birth. Feminists believed that their shared sisterhood fundamentally connected them across class, racial, and national differences, which is only partly true as the modern feminist fight tended to neglect the concept of race to begin with.[127] Women unintentionally oppressed each other despite believing that they were in the fight together. Believing in sisterhood and solidarity often went against the belief in class importance/structure.

Based on the abundance of self-contradictions and splits within the feminist movement, one must always ask what the intentions of modern evaluations are (for example, the modern readings of Austin). For example, the second wave of feminists was perhaps, as Le Goff pointed out in *Reconstructing the Past*, utilizing "the undefinable residue of historical analysis" with regard to the

---

[124] Cott, *Feminist Struggles*, 166-167.
[125] Ibid., 167.
[126] Ibid., 181.
[127] Ibid., 168.

history of mentalities.[128] The history of mentalities was applied to literature and enhanced in a way that served the modern movement. The assumption that all political intentions in Austin's literature were gender-driven is false because it does not take into consideration the non-sex-based political purposes. The origins of feminism as a movement are broad, as it varies from one geographical place to another; for example, the rise of the movement in the 1960s was for the liberation of women in Western countries. Capitalism was undergoing transformations that affected women considerably.

Of particular importance was the role of women in the labor force, which would be too limiting to apply to Austin, because despite labor being among the causes she worked for (both partaking in it and improving its availability and quality for all), she was more politically inclined. The author not only encouraged women to get jobs, she also critiqued the system that did not already have that in place, which is why we witness her encouraging women to insert themselves into whatever professional skills and occupations were available.[129] It was as much about making a statement as it was about earning a wage.

What one can ultimately gather is that the feminists of the 1960s and 1970s were creating new traditions by using previous events, turning to history, and (re-)interpreting events and people. However, it is important to be critical of this, because not all history that is brought up for modern interpretation was indeed as it is perceived in re-readings. An 'invented tradition' means a set of practices, normally governed by overtly or tacitly accepted rules, of a ritual or symbolic nature, which seek to inculcate certain values and norms of behavior by repetition, which automatically implies continuity with the past.[130] On the matter of the past, as Hobsbawm and Ranger define it, we can see that the female scholars of the 1960s and 1970s strived both for more inclusion for what they had to say and for more mentions of women in the grand picture of history.

Mary Hunter Austin was an author, but first and foremost she was a socialist and a critical voice in regard to the political system, especially during the First World War. Thus, one must ask: was she indeed a feminist according to the definition of a feminist in its modern understanding? More so within modern analysis than the author's original intent, as she was more of a spirited artist

---

[128] Jacques Le Goff and Pierre Nora, eds., *Constructing the Past: Essays in Historical Methodology* (Cambridge: Cambridge University Press), 166.
[129] Mary Austin, "Young Woman and Her Part in War," *The Knoxville Independent*, June 29, 1918, 7.
[130] Hobsbawm, *The Invention of Tradition*, 2-5.

for collective growth than the holder of a 'women above all else' agenda (for example, she chose to leave women's clubs because they were limiting). The reconstruction of the past is a methodology that is collectively used in historical analysis.[131] Much like the growth of gender history within gender studies (and the feminist liberation movement), "what we call the past is merely a function and production of a continuous present and its discourses."[132] What is collectively agreed upon by scholars is that the basic principle behind all connective structures is repetition, and memory of the past is brought to the present through explanations of tradition.[133] In this case, the intention was to create a feminist tradition through the reinterpretation of Austin.

However, this is where one might meet a set of problems, the first being the process of the quantities of these systems and information. Are modern feminists justified in their analysis? The geographical and quantitative units by which groups are defined, in this case Austin's literature, must have both quantity and quality: judging the entirety of her literary output on just three works can possibly lead to falsification.[134] Thus, answering the question of whether gender is something that one has or something that one is, which is the basis from which Austin's feminism is translated to appeal to modern norms and new ideas, stands too weak.

One can claim that modern interpretations, such as those of Butler mentioned above, were not the direct intentions of Austin; the reason for this is that women in the earlier 1900s wanted empowerment as women, not to be empowered as superior, which is not to say that superiority is a feminist demand, as it is not, but modern feminism includes many more factors than just equality for the two biological sexes. As previously mentioned, Assmann claims that strength and weakness in tradition come from the presence of repetition (or lack thereof),[135] which is used as a tool. The historian Ola Stugu writes about identity in *Historie i Bruk*, analyzing the common link between history and identity.[136] Stugu discusses the perception that history (and that having one) affects identity, again going back to the concept of memory and how collective memory creates collective identity, and he conclusively presents the idea that it creates stronger communities (even if some of the

---

[131] Halbwachs, *On Collective Memory*, 46-48.
[132] Offen, "Defining Feminism," 9.
[133] Assmann, *Cultural Memory*, 3.
[134] Ibid., 12-13.
[135] Ibid., 234-236.
[136] Ola Svein Stugu, *Historie i Bruk*, 2nd ed. (Oslo: Samlaget, 2008), 34-39.

history is reconstructions or "myths").[137] Assmann agrees to an extent when he states that "whereas knowledge has a universalist perspective, a tendency toward generalization and standardization, memory, even cultural memory, is local, egocentric, and specific to a group and its values."[138]

Based on the comparisons made here, it is clear that the impact of the First World War on the writer created a more politically driven proto-feminist agency than a feminist agency solely for the sake of gender norm-related issues; her objectives were more about ensuring democracy and how women could contribute to this. She valued women for what they could do in the fight rather than what they 'could not do' because society claimed it was for men. Her literary works between 1914 and 1920 were culturally valuable pieces from the beginning, and it was only after later re-interpretations that they were deemed truly feminist.

Overall, Mary Hunter Austin could be classified as a suffragette, a socialist proto-feminist of the 1910s and 1920s who was later reinvented as a feminist in the 1960s and 1970s. Like any other hero of the past, memory was essential for the creation of such an image, although it was not a historical but rather an idealist one, resembling the wishes and needs of a movement willing to look for its own tradition in the past. There, they would eventually find Austin, whose demands were revolutionary in her own times and therefore even more fitting for re-interpretation according to the feminist narrative of the second wave of feminism in the United States.

Feminism, the suffrage movement, activism, and politics aside, Austin was a pioneer, who wrote about things she knew and questioned everything to evolve in many ways as she went on. Marcia Muth (1919-2014) writes in the 2007 foreword to Austin's *The American Rhythm, Studies and Re-expressions of Amerindian Songs* that "'Pioneer Women' conjure up a ready image ... above all else, it calls for the image of determination,"[139] which she deems to be a title worthy for Austin. "There have always been pioneer women and in each generation that tradition continues,"[140] Muth adds, echoing the concepts of tradition, creation, the bringing forward of them, and Austin's role within

---

[137] Ibid., 34-39. For further reading on the ideas about the contrast between 'truth' and 'falsity' in relation to memory, see Steven D. Brown and Paula Reavey, "False Memories and Real Epistemic Problems," *Culture & Psychology* 23, no. 2 (2017): 171.
[138] Assmann, "Communicative and Cultural Memory," 113.
[139] Marcia Muth, "Foreword," in Mary Austin, *The American Rhythm, Studies and Re-expressions of Amerindian Songs* (Santa Fe: Sunstone Press, 2007 [Facsimile of 1930 ed.]), ii.
[140] Ibid.

them. The step of first creating significance becomes more evident once the scientific links become sharper in order "to identify the most obvious and crucial centers of national memory, and then to reveal the existence of invisible bonds tying them all together,"[141] and then to combine this significance with the strength of tradition.

---

[141] Nora, "Preface," xiii.

Conclusion

In 1935, a year after Mary Hunter Austin's death, the journalist Arthur E. Dubois wrote that the "limits of what she might become were set by the group or ideal or cult or country [to] which she wished to belong."[1] Based on this, it is correct to argue that the ways in which Austin herself, feminists (of various periods), and various other groups approached the author are left to subjective analysis. Austin was without question a fighter on behalf of herself and womankind; nevertheless, she also fought as a true citizen and was not just limited to being a woman. She was eclectic and open to change, which leaves Dubois describing her as someone who never truly knew in which direction she was going.[2] But she never stopped.

Austin, both personally and professionally, was in many ways chaotic, and her literature, the result of her experiences written at the time of a global war, only ever gained the analytical appreciation it truly deserved once readers took a step back and gained a better perspective of the narratives. Austin was memorable to those she encountered, and she continues to be memorable to those who read her work a hundred years later. There is a very clear shift in how the political environment in the United States before, during, and after the First World War impacted the author's ideas and philosophies: from her pacifist stance to the changes to her criticism of men's warfare, encouragement of female labor and the fight for equal citizenship that resulted in her being more open to the idea of a war that was to serve the greater good (democracy). Austin's associations with the suffrage movement also require further investigation in order to understand why she went from being 'radical' to not wanting to be associated with the limitations of women's groups, because this is perhaps something that she was not experiencing alone; was she 'above' them, or did it hurt her personal feelings that they would "correct her and hold her back," as she recalled in *Earth Horizon*?

The Ford, The Young Woman Citizen, "Sex Emancipation Through War," and *No. 26 Jayne Street* were all directly affected and inspired by the First World War, despite the stories and ideas lingering in the author's mind prior to it (e.g. her opinions on various matters quoted in different newspaper articles long before they were published as books and essays and in the events of *The*

---

[1] Dubois, "Mary Hunter Austin," 238.
[2] Ibid.

Ford). Austin's ideas and characters have modern outlooks on life and society, challenging the norm, which is refreshing to put it lightly. An element that is constant in all of her stories, and a reflection of herself and who she 'wished' to be, is the strong female characters. The women in her stories are not trying to be more than society allows an individual to be – they are only trying to be equal to what they should be (i.e. the equals of men).

From her autobiography to *A Woman of Genius, The Ford, No. 26 Jayne Street*, the political essays, and so on, we see norms being defined in a quest for equality – equality in the sense of social justice. Austin's strength and refreshing personality and art derived from her personal unrest and her refusal to settle for the standards that society had set for her at the time through her education, imagination, and eventually divorce (which in itself was highly radical, and uncommon, at the time), before going on to write about breaking the standards for what a traditional marriage should be.

After the First World War, one can notice a great shift in the way that Austin becomes more driven on a personal level. She focuses her work on personal development and, among other things, giving lectures rather than fighting the cause on the street in a more hands-on fashion, as she did at the peak of her activism. Consequently, she then shifted her focus on her lectures in order to remain relevant in terms of her literature (therefore also producing more). Austin's attention also turned back to her concern with Native American rights, which can be argued either to be the result of her moving back to relevant regions or to be the reason that she moved back because she wished to continue concerning herself with what she had started out with in her earlier years.

Austin, when she was in her forties and beyond, was well aware that she had left her mark on American literature and culture and carried her impact with pride. She experienced many shifts in her lifetime both on a personal and literary level, never 'only' settling for the cards she was dealt with in life. This showcases her versatility and wonderfully eclectic energy that saw many ups and downs, but which was ultimately re-discovered to make a mark once again. She had an eagerness to evolve intellectually, financially, socially, and politically beyond the geographical limits of Carlinville, Illinois and the social and emotional limits of life that were intended for her as the daughter of a single mother.

To claim that the author was out of the ordinary is not an exaggeration, and, as mentioned in the biographical chapter, the post-World War narrative gave her new life with the growth of the concept of modern feminism and the new gender roles at the time. However, claiming Austin's intentions as predominantly feminist would be limiting, as the writer and activist made universal attempts to change society, especially according to socialist ideas.

Ultimately, what one can gather is that she strived for social change not only on women's behalf but wherever she saw injustice. Two of the most important reasons why Mary Hunter Austin's significance did not truly come to a feminist light until many years later could potentially be because, first, her most important political works were published at a time when society was handling larger issues, and thus an appreciation of her narratives was not fully discovered until much later, and second, her influence on modern interpretations was entirely subjective to modern-day feminist readings and re-interpretations. Austin's stronger political agenda is clearly what was most spoken of in some geographical areas, such as Washington, DC. In places such as New York, there was something of a lack of long, in-depth political articles about Austin in that period, indicating that a greater quantity focused on cultural aspects rather than political ones (though this is not to say that political aspects were not in focus). Austin was a social critic above all else, and it was this political criticism that was taken in the 1960s and 1970s and re-defined to include a full-bodied feminism rather than the early 'feminist' definition that was in its infancy during Austin's life. However, subjective power is what gives collective impact and influence, and that is what Austin had and continues to have.

The history of mentalities allowed interpretations that were based on vagueness in order to assist the modern feminist narrative further. The vagueness of mental history and cultural memory came together in order to function as a tool when the feminist tradition was being written in the age of women's liberation. The reconstructed memorization serves a purpose, and, as Gro Hagemann argues, the line between women's (and feminist) history and social history is often blurred. Even Austin's own literature is impacted by vagueness and memory; for example, *The Ford*'s main story is inspired by true events, however it is also imbued with a happier ending and a more optimistic story. The characters are inspired by Austin's own wish to be viewed as well established.

She was not a feminist to begin with, at least not according to the modern definition, as much as she was a social and political critic – but she perhaps *became* one kind of feminist in her later life. Her dedication to literature and women's strength shone through in her books, but was her personal perception of the world more than an agenda? Austin was a feminist as far as a prototype feminist goes; she was in the suffrage movement but chose to eventually leave, as it was limiting to her. Modern feminists' interpretations of Mary Hunter Austin's literature and person are not entirely objective, as they have chosen parts that appealed to them rather than the whole picture. The essays viewed as feminist manifestos were more a question of citizenship for all citizens but, at that particular time, especially for women, as they did not have the same opportunity to speak and claim rights. Based on the comparisons that have been made in the present volume, it is clear that the impact of the First World War on the late writer stimulated a politically driven proto-feminism rather than feminism for the sake of gender equality and an end to patriarchic rule; her objectives were more geared toward ensuring democracy and showing how women could contribute to this. She valued women for what they could do in the fight rather than what they could not do because society claimed it was for men. Mary Hunter Austin wanted equality, and her modern readers see this as a fight for liberation; however, women's equality does not necessarily mean feminist liberation. To say that modern feminists are wrong would not be correct, and while it would be correct to claim that historical vagueness served in an assisting way, that is the case with most analytical history. The security of an already well-established movement contributed to strengthening the union and development of a modern feminist identity and a sense of belonging through shared beliefs. Through re-readings, the anchoring of a rich history of strong individual agency makes a contribution to collective identity and agency.

Most important of all, while the findings in this book have only begun to scratch at the surface of Austin's life and works, they lay a methodological ground for further scientific research and examinations of the author's life and impact through close readings.

Works Cited

Archival Sources

Elizabeth Garver Jordan Papers, New York Public Library, Rare Books and Manuscripts Division.

Newspapers and Periodicals

L'Italia
The Arizona Republican
The Chicago Eagle
The Day Book
The Evening Star
The Evening Times (Iowa)
The Evening World
The Glasgow Courier
The Idaho Republican
The Knoxville Independent
The New York Herald
The New York Tribune
The New Republic
The News Scimitar
The Rock Island Argus
The Rock Island Argus and Daily Union
The Seattle Star
The Sun
The Sunday Star
The Washington Herald
The Washington Times

Secondary Works

Adams, Ansel. "Notes to Mary Austin." In *Mary Hunter Austin: A Centennial Booklet Published by the Mary Austin Home.* Independence, CA: Mary Austin Home, 1968.

Addams, Jane. *Democracy and Social Ethics.* New York: Macmillan, 1902.

Adickes, Sandra. *To Be Young Was Very Heaven: Women in New York Before the Great War.* London: Macmillan, 1997.

Alaimo, Stacey. "The Undomesticated Nature of Feminism: Mary Austin and the Progressive Women Conservationists." *Studies in American Fiction* 26, no. 1 (1998): 73-96.

Alexander, Sally. "Women, Class and Sexual Differences in the 1830s and 1840s: Some Reflections on the Writing of a Feminist History." *History Workshop*, no. 17 (1984): 125-149.

Altman, Dorothy J. "Mary Hunter Austin and the Roles of Women." PhD diss., State University of New York at Albany, 1979.

Antler, Joyce. "Feminism as Life-Process: The Life and Career of Lucy Sprague Mitchell." In *Feminist Struggles for Sex Equality: The History of Women in the United States*, vol. 20, edited by Nancy F. Cott, 196-219. Munich: Saur, 1994.

Armitage, Shelly. Review of *Mary Austin's Regionalism: Reflections on Gender, Genre, and Geography*, by Heike Schaefer. *Tulsa Studies in Women's Literature* 25, no. 1 (2006): 170-172.

Assmann, Jan. "Communicative and Cultural Memory." In *Cultural Memory Studies: An International and Interdisciplinary Handbook*, edited by Astrid Erll and Ansgar Nünning, 109-118. Berlin: De Gruyter, 2008.

———. *Cultural Memory and Early Civilization*. New York: Cambridge University Press, 2012.

Austin, Mary. *The American Rhythm, Studies and Re-expressions of Amerindian Songs*. Edited by Marcia Muth. Facsimile of 1930. Santa Fe: Sunstone Press, 2007.

———. *Beyond Borders: The Selected Essays of Mary Austin*. Edited by Reuben J. Ellis. Carbondale, IL: Southern Illinois University Press, 1997.

———. *Cactus Thorn*. Reno, NV: University of Nevada Press, 1994.

———. "The Conversion of Ah Lew Sing." *The Overland Monthly* 30 (October 1897): 307-312.

———. *Earth Horizon: An Autobiography*. Boston/New York: Houghton Mifflin, 1932.

———. *The Ford*. Boston/New York: Houghton Mifflin, 1917.

———. *The Land of Little Rain*. Boston/New York: Houghton Mifflin, 1903.

———. *The Man Jesus: Being a Brief Account of the Life and Teaching of the Prophet of Nazareth*. New York: Harper & Brothers, 1915.

———. "The Mother of Felipe." *The Overland Monthly* 20 (November 1892): 534-538.

———. *No. 26 Jayne Street*. Boston/New York: Houghton Mifflin, 1920.

———. *One Hundred Miles on Horseback*. California: Dawson's Book Shop, 1963.

———. *A Woman of Genius*. New York: Doubleday, Page & Company, 1912.

———. *The Young Woman Citizen*. New York: The Woman's Press, 1918.

Bebel, August. *Woman and Socialism*. New York: Socialist Literature Company, 1910.

Beneria, Lourdes. "Conceptualizing the Labor Force: The Underestimation of Women's Economic Activities." *The Journal of Development Studies* 17, no. 3 (1981): 10-28.

Beneria, Lourdes, Günseli Berik and Maria S. Floro. *Género, Desarrollo y Globalización: Una Visión desde la economía feminista*. Barcelona: Routledge, 2018.

Bennett, Scott H. *Radical Pacifism: The War Resisters League and Gandhian Nonviolence in America, 1915-1963*. Syracuse, NY: Syracuse University Press, 2003.

Bernhard, Michael, Tiago Fernandes and Rui Branco. "Civil Society and Democracy in an Era of Inequality." *Comparative Politics* 49, no. 3 (2017): 297-309.

Berry, J. Wilkes. "Mary Hunter Austin (1868-1934)." *American Literary Realism, 1870-1910* 2, no. 2 (1969): 125-131.

Berson, Robin Kadison. *Jane Addams: A Biography*. Westport, CT: Greenwood Press, 2004.

Bingham, Edwin R. "American Wests through Autobiography and Memoir." *Pacific Historical Review* 56, no. 1 (1987): 1-24.

Blend, Benay. "Mary Austin and the Western Conservation Movement: 1900-1927." *Journal of the Southwest* 30, no. 1 (1988): 12-34.

Bøe, Jan Bjarne and Ketil Knutsen. *Innføring i Historiebruk*. Oslo: Cappelen Damm Høyskoleforlaget, 2013.

Brittain, Vera. *Testament of Youth*. London: Fontana/Virago, 1979.

Brosman, Catharine Savage. *Southwestern Women Writers and The Vision of Goodness*. Jefferson, NC: McFarland, 2016.

Brown, Steven D. and Paula Reavey. "False Memories and Real Epistemic Problems." *Culture & Psychology* 23, no. 2 (2017): 171-185.

Bryson, Valerie. *Feminist Political Theory: An Introduction*. New York: Palgrave Macmillan, 2003.

Butler, Judith. *Gender Trouble*. New York/London: Routledge, 2006.

Caine, Barbara and Anne Summers. "Suffragettes to Social Media: Waves of Feminism." Lecture, Sydney Opera House, Sydney, March 4, 2018.

Castro, Ginette. *American Feminism: A Contemporary History*. New York: New York University Press, 1990.

Coffman, Edward M. *The War to End All Wars: The American Military Experience in World War I*. New York: Oxford University Press, 1986.

Cook, Nancy. Review of *Exploring Lost Borders: Critical Essays on Mary Austin*, by Melody Graulich and Elizabeth Klimasmith. *Western Historical Quarterly* 32, no. 1 (2001): 96-97.

Cott, Nancy F., ed. *Feminist Struggles for Sex Equality: The History of Women in the United States*, vol. 20. Munich: Saur, 1994.

Dell, Floyd. *Women as World Builders: Studies in Modern Feminism*. Chicago: Forbes and Company, 1913.

——. *Homecoming: An Autobiography*. New York: Farrar & Rinehart, 1933.

Dodge Luhan, Mabel. *Movers and Shakers*. Albuquerque: University of New Mexico Press, 1985.

Downs, Laura Lee "War Work." In *The Cambridge History of the First World War*, vol. 3: *Civil Society*, edited by Jay Winter, 72-95. Cambridge: Cambridge University Press, 2014.

Dubbs, Chris. *An Unladylike Profession: American Women War Correspondents in World War I*. Lincoln, NE: University of Nebraska Press, 2020.

DuBois, Arthur E. "Mary Hunter Austin 1968-1934." *Southwest Review* 20, no. 3 (1935): 231-264.

Dumenil, Lynn. *The Second Line of Defense: American Women and World War I.* Chapel Hill: University of North Carolina Press, 2017.

Edwards, Lee R. and Arlyn Diamond. *American Voices, American Women.* New York: Avon, 1973.

Filipowicz, Halina. "'Am I That Name?' Feminism, Feminist Criticism, and Gender Studies." *The Polish Review* 59, no. 1 (2014): 3-15.

Fink, Augusta. *I-Mary: A Biography of Mary Austin.* Tucson, AZ: University of Arizona Press, 1983.

Fitzgerald, F. Scott. *Tender Is the Night.* New York: Cambridge University Press, 2012.

Foucault, Michel. *Language, Counter-memory, Practice: Selected Essays and Interviews.* Edited by Donald F. Bouchard. New York: Cornell University Press, 1980.

Freedman, Lawrence. *War.* New York: Oxford University Press, 1994.

Friedman, Michelle, Jo Metelerkamp and Ros Posel. "What is Feminism? And What Kind of Feminist Am I?" *Agenda: Empowering Women for Gender Equity* 1 (1987): 3-24.

Funk, Ann. Review of *A Mary Austin Reader*, by Esther Lanigan. *The Antioch Review* 54, no. 4 (1996): 493-494.

Fussell, Paul. *The Great War and Modern Memory.* New York: Oxford University Press, 1975.

Gabrielson, Teena, "Woman-Thought, Social Capital, and the Generative State: Mary Austin and the Integrative Civic Ideal in Progressive Thought." *American Journal of Political Science* 50, no. 3 (2006): 650-663.

Gavin, Lettie. *American Women In World War I: They Also Served.* Boulder, CO: University Press of Colorado, 2011.

Gelfant, Blanche H. "'Lives' of Women Writers: Cather, Austin, Porter / and Willa, Mary, Katherine Anne." *NOVEL: A Forum on Fiction* 18, no. 1 (1984): 64-80.

Gersdorf, Catrin. *The Poetics and Politics of the Desert Landscape and the Construction of America.* New York: Rodopi, 2009.

Gilbert, Sandra M. "Soldier's Heart: Literary Men, Literary Women, and the Great War." *Signs* 8, no. 3 (1983): 422-450.

Goldman, Emma. *Anarchism and Other Essays.* 2nd ed. New York: Mother Earth Publishing Association, 1911.

Goodman, Susan and Carl Dawson. *Mary Austin and the American West.* Berkeley/Los Angeles: University of California Press, 2009.

Graulich, Melody. "Mary, Mary, Quite Contrary." *The Women's Review of Books* 1, no. 4 (1984): 16-17.

Graulich, Melody and Elizabeth Klimasmith, eds. *Exploring Lost Borders: Critical Essays on Mary Austin.* Reno, NV: University of Nevada Press, 1999.

Grayzel, Susan R. "Men and Women at Home." In *The Cambridge History of the First World War*, vol. 3: *Civil Society*, edited by Jay Winter, 96-120. Cambridge: Cambridge University Press, 2014.

———. *Women and the First World War.* New York: Routledge, 2013.

Green, Anna and Kathleen Troup. *The Houses of History: A Critical Reader in Twentieth-Century History and Theory.* Manchester: Manchester University Press, 1999.

Gregory, Ross. *The Origins of American Intervention in the First World War.* New York: Norton & Company, Inc., 1972.

Griffiths, Morwenna. *Feminisms and the Self: The Web of Identity.* New York: Routledge, 1996.

Gunnell, John G. *Political Theory: Tradition and Interpretation.* Cambridge, MA: Winthrop, 1979.

Hagemann, Gro. *Feminisme Og Historieskriving.* Oslo: Universitetsforlaget, 2001.

Hahn, Emily. *Mable.* New York: Houghton Mifflin Company, 1977.

———. *Romanic Rebels: An Informal History of Bohemianism in America.* New York: Houghton Mifflin Company, 1967.

Halbwachs, Maurice. *On Collective Memory.* Edited by Lewis A. Coser. Chicago: University of Chicago Press, 1992.

Hall, Stuart. *Encoding and Decoding in the Television Discourse.* Birmingham: Centre for Contemporary Cultural Studies, 1973.

Hallett, Christine E. *Veiled Warriors: Allied Nurses of the First World War.* Oxford: Oxford University Press, 2014.

Hastedt, Glenn P. *Spies, Wiretaps, and Secret Operations: An Encyclopedia of American Espionage.* Santa Barbara, CA: ABC-Clio, 2011.

Hemingway, Ernest. *A Farewell to Arms: The Hemingway Library Edition.* New York: Scribner, 2014.

Hill, Mary A. "Charlotte Perkins Gilman: A Feminist Struggle With Womanhood." In *Feminist Struggles for Sex Equality: The History of Women in the United States*, vol. 20, edited by Nancy F. Cott, 142-165. Munich: Saur, 1994.

Hirsch, Marianne and Valerie Smith. "Feminism and Cultural Memory: An Introduction." *Signs* 28, no. 1 (2002): 1-19.

Hobsbawm, Eric and Terence Ranger, eds. *The Invention of Tradition.* Cambridge: Cambridge University Press, 2000.

Hoffman, Abraham. "Mary Austin, Stafford Austin, and the Owens Valley." *Journal of the Southwest* 53, no. 2/3 (2011): 305-322.

Holub, Robert C. *Reception Theory.* New York: Routledge, 2003.

Howard, Michael. *The First World War: A Very Short Introduction.* New York: Oxford University Press, 2002.

Hsu, Hsuan L. *Geography and the Production of Space in Nineteenth-Century American Literature.* New York: Cambridge University Press, 2010.

Jacob, Frank, Jeffrey Shaw, and Timothy Demy, eds. *War and the Humanities: The Cultural Impact of the First World War.* Paderborn: Schöningh/Brill, 2018.

Jauss, Hans-Robert. *Toward an Aesthetic of Reception.* Minneapolis: University of Minnesota Press, 1982.

Johnson, Jeffrey A. "Aliens, Enemy Aliens, and Minors: Anti-Radicalism and the Jewish Left," in *Historicizing Fear: Ignorance, Vilification, and Othering*, edited by Travis D. Boyce and Winsome M. Chunnu, 193-206. Boulder, CO: University Press of Colorado, 2020.

Kennedy, David M. *Over Here: The First World War and American Society.* New York: Oxford University Press, 1980.

Kingsland, Sharon E. "The Battling Botanist: Daniel Trembly MacDougal, Mutation Theory, and the Rise of Experimental Evolutionary Biology in America, 1900-1912." *Isis* 82, no. 3 (1991): 479-509.

Kurtz, Lester, ed. *Encyclopedia of Violence, Peace, and Conflict.* Fairfax: Academic Press, 1999.

Lance, Derril Keith Curry. "The Suffragette Movement in Great Britain: A Study of the Factors Influencing the Strategy Choices of the Women's Social and Political Union, 1913-1918." MA thesis, University of North Texas, 1977.

Langlois, Karen S. "A Fresh Voice from the West: Mary Austin, California, and American Literary Magazines, 1892-1910." *California History* 69, no. 1 (1990): 22-35.

———. "Mary Austin and Andrew Forbes: Poetry, Photography, and the Eastern Sierra." *California History* 85, no. 1 (2007): 24-43.

———. "Mary Hunter Austin and Lincoln Steffens." *Huntington Library Quarterly* 49, no. 4 (1986): 357-383.

Le Goff, Jacques. "Mentalities: A History of Ambiguities." In *Constructing the Past*, edited by Jacques Le Goff and Pierre Nora, 166-180. New York: Cambridge University Press, 2011.

Le Goff, Jacques and Pierre Nora, eds. *Constructing the Past: Essays in Historical Methodology.* Cambridge: Cambridge University Press, 2011.

Leed, Eric. *No Man's Land: Combat and Identity in World War I.* New York: Cambridge University Press, 1979.

Lewin, Ellen. *Feminist Anthropology: A Reader.* Hoboken, NJ: John Wiley & Sons, 2009.

Lindsey, Linda L. *Gender Roles: A Sociological Perspective.* 5th ed. Boston: Pearson Education, 2011.

Luckmann, Thomas. "Remarks on Personal Identity: Inner, Social and Historical Time." In *Identity: Personal and Socio-Cultural*, edited by Anita Jacobson-Widding, 67-91. Atlantic Highlands, NJ: Humanities, 1983.

Lynn, Kenneth S. "The Rebels of Greenwich Village." *Perspectives in American History* 8 (1974): 335-380.

Maffi, Mario. *Gateway to the Promised Land: Ethnic Cultures on New York's Lower East Side.* New York: New York University Press, 1995.

Malesevic, Sinisa. *Sociology of War and Violence.* New York: Cambridge University Press, 2010.

Marshall, Catherine. *Militarism versus Feminism.* London: Virago, 1987.

Maxwell, Angie and Todd Shields. *The Legacy of Second-Wave Feminism in American Politics.* Cham: Springer, 2018.

McLaren, Margaret A. "Two Feminist Views on the Self, Identity and Collective Action." *Hypatia* 14, no. 1 (1999): 120-125.

Merriman, John. *Modern Europe from the Renaissance to the Present.* New York: Yale University Press, 1996.

Meyer, G. J. *The World Remade America in World War I.* New York: Bantam Books, 2016.

Mill, John Stuart. *The Subjection of Women*. Indianapolis: Hackett Publishing Company, 1988.

Miller, Sally M. "For White Men Only: The Socialist Party of America and Issues of Gender, Ethnicity and Race." *The Journal of the Gilded Age and Progressive Era* 2, no. 3 (2003): 283-302.

Mohammed, Jowan A. "Mary Hunter Austin und die Forderungen nach einer Veraenderung der Geschlechterrollen in den USA, 1914-1918." In *Geschlecht und Klassenkampf: Die „Frauenfrage" aus deutscher und internationaler Perspektive im 19. und 20. Jahrhundert*, edited by Vincent Streichhahn and Frank Jacob, 222-239. Berlin: Metropol Verlag, 2020.

Montefiore, Dora B. *The Position of Women in the Socialist Movement*. London: Twentieth Century Press, 1909.

Muth, Marcia. "Foreword." In Mary Austin, *The American Rhythm, Studies and Re-expressions of Amerindian Songs*, i-iii. Santa Fe: Sunstone Press, 2007 [1930].

Neumann, Johanna. *And Yet They Persisted: How American Women Won the Right to Vote*. Hoboken, NJ: John Wiley and Sons, 2020.

New York State Writers Institute. "Elaine Showalter." Accessed May 5, 2019. https://www.albany.edu/writers-inst/webpages4/archives/showalter_elaine 09.html.

Nora, Pierre. "Preface to English Language Edition: From Lieux de Memorie to Realms of Memory." In *Realms of Memory: Rethinking the French Past*, edited by Pierre Nora and Lawrence D. Kritzman, translated by Arthur Goldhammer, xv-xxiv. New York: Colombia University Press, 1996.

Norwood, Vera L. "Heroines of Nature: Four Women Respond to the American Landscape." *Environmental Review* 8, no. 1 (1984): 34-56.

Offen, Karen. "Defining Feminism: A Comparative Historical Approach." *Signs* 14, no. 1 (1988): 119-120.

Peterson, John. "The Interconnected Bioregion: Transregional Networks in Mary Austin's *The Ford*." *Western American Literature: A Journal of Literary, Cultural, and Place Studies* 52, no. 1 (2017): 157-78.

——. "Wrestling with 'Half Gods': Biblical Discourse in Mary Austin's *The Ford*." *Christianity & Literature* 67, no. 4 (2018): 653-668.

Plain, Gill and Susan Sellers. *A History of Feminist Literary Criticism*. Cambridge: Cambridge University Press, 2012.

Portolés, Asunción Oliva. *Miradas Feministas: Del Postcolonialismo a La Globalización*. Madrid: Pulmen S.L.L., 2016.

Potter, Jane. "'I begin to feel as a normal being should, in spite of the blood and anguish in which I move': American Women's First World War Nursing Memoirs." In *First World War Nursing: New Perspectives*, edited by Alison S. Fell and Christine E. Hallett, 51-68. New York: Routledge, 2013.

Powell, Lawrence Clark. "A Dedication to the Memory of Mary Hunter Austin 1868-1934." *Arizona and the West* 10, no. 1 (1968): 1-4.

Pribanic-Smith, Erika J. and Jared Schroeder. *Emma Goldman's No-Conscription League and the First Amendment*. New York: Routledge, 2018

Rappaport, Helen, ed. *Encyclopedia of Women Social Reformers*. Santa Barbara, CA: ABC-Clio, 2001.

Riley, Glenda. "'Wimmin Is Everywhere': Conserving and Feminizing Western Landscapes, 1870 to 1940." *Western Historical Quarterly* 29, no. 1 (1998): 4-23.

——. *Women and Nature: Saving the "Wild" West*. Lincoln, NE: University of Nebraska Press, 1999.

Robb, George and W. Brian Newsome. "Introduction: Rethinking World War I: Occupation, Liberation, and Reconstruction." *Economic and Political Weekly* 3, no. 35 (August-September 2010): 50-57.

Rose, Sonya O. *What Is Gender History?* Malden, MA: Polity Press, 2010.

Rudnick, Lois. "Feminist on the Frontier." Review of *Mary Austin: Songs of a Maverick*, by Esther Lanigan Stineman. *The Women's Review of Books* 7, no. 7 (1990): 22.

Rupert, James. "Mary Austin's Landscape Line in Native American Literature." *Southwest Review* 68, no 4. (1983): 376-390.

Schaefer, Oleh Heike. *Mary Austin's Regionalism: Reflections on Gender, Genre, and Geography*. Charlottesville, VA: University of Virginia Press, 2004.

Schneider, Dorothy and Carl J. Schneider. *Into the Breach: American Women Overseas in World War I*. New Zealand: Penguin Books, 1991.

Scott, Joan W. "Gender: A Useful Category in Historical Analysis." *The American Historical Review* 91, no. 5 (1986): 1053-1075.

Seymour, Richard. *American Insurgents: A Brief History of American Anti-Imperialism*. Chicago: Haymarket Books, 2012.

Showalter, Elaine. *These Modern Women: Autobiographical Essays from the Twenties*. New York: The Feminist Press, 1989.

Siskin, Clifford and William Warren, eds. *This Is Enlightenment*. Chicago: University of Chicago Press, 2010.

Smith, Angela K. *The Second Battlefield: Women, Modernism and the First World War*. Manchester: Manchester University Press, 2000.

Spivak, Gayatri Chakravorty. *The Post-Colonial Critic: Interviews, Strategies, Dialogues*. Edited by Sara Harasym. New York: Chapman and Hall, 2014.

Stineman, Esther Lanigan. *Mary Austin: Song of a Maverick*. New Haven: Yale University Press, 1989.

——. "Mary Austin Rediscovered." *Journal of the Southwest* 30, no. 4 (1988): 545-551.

Stout, Janis P. "Mary Austin's Feminism: A Reassessment." *Studies in the Novel* 30, no. 1 (1998): 77-101.

Streichhahn, Vincent and Frank Jacob, eds. *Geschlecht und Klassenkampf: Die "Frauenfrage" aus deutscher und internationaler Perspektive im 19. und 20. Jahrhundert*. Berlin: Metropol, 2020.

Stugu, Ola Svein. *Historie i Bruk*. 2nd ed. Oslo: Samlaget, 2008.

Sullivan, Gwen. Review of *Mary Austin's Southwest: An Anthology of Her Literary Criticism*, by Chelsea Blackbird and Barney Nelson. *Rocky Mountain Review of Language and Literature* 60, no. 1 (2006): 126-128.

Thompson, Martyn P. "Reception Theory and the Interpretation of Historical Meaning." *History and Theory* 32, no. 3 (1993), 248-272.

UMass Amherst Libraries. "Arlyn, Diamond, 1941-." Accessed May 5, 2019. http://scua.library.umass.edu/umarmot/diamond-arlyn-1941/.

Van Doren, Carl. *Contemporary American Novelists (1900-1920)*. Salt Lake City, UT: Project Gutenberg Literary Archive Foundation, 2009.
Vander Hook, Sue. *The United States Enters World War I*. Minnesota: Abdo Publishing, 2010.
Venzon, Anne Cipriano, ed. *The United States in the First World War: An Encyclopedia*. New York: Routledge, 2012.
Visweswaran, Kamala. "Histories of Feminist Ethnography." *Annual Review of Anthropology* 26 (1997): 591-621.
Ware, Susan. *American Women's History: A Very Short Introduction*. Oxford: Oxford University Press.
Weir, Allison. *Sacrificial Logics: Feminist Theory and the Critique of Identity*. New York: Routledge, 1996.
Wellek, Rene and Austin Warren. *Theory of Literature*. 3rd ed. Harmondsworth: Penguin Books, 1963.
Wilson, Ross J. *New York and the First World War*. Farnham: Ashgate, 2014.
Winter, Jay. *Remembering War: The Great War Between Memory and History in the Twentieth Century*. New Haven, CT: Yale University Press, 2006.
Wright, Elizabeth. "Mary Hunter Austin (1868-1934)." In *American Women Writers 1900-1945: A Bio-Bibliographical Critical Sourcebook*, edited by Laurie Champion, 13-19. Westport, CT: Greenwood Publishing Group, 2000.
Wynn, Dudley Taylor. "A Critical Study of the Writings of Mary Austin (1868-1934)." PhD diss., Graduate School of Arts and Science of New York University, 1941.
Zieger, Robert H. *America's Great War: World War I and the American Experience*. New York: Rowman & Littlefield Publishers, Inc., 2001.

Index

A

Activism
  Rallies, xi, 16, 33, 59, 65, 85-86
  Demonstrations, 16, 67, 68, 87
  Volunteering, 14, 38, 46, 51-53, 63, 80
  Food drive and conservation, 53, 63
Adams, Ansel, 30
Addams, Jane, 50
Austin, Ruth, 1, 8, 9, 10, 11, 20
Austin, Stafford Wallace, xiii, xvii, 1, 6, 7, 8, 9, 11, 18, 59, 60

B

Brother. *See* Hunter, Jim, 2, 4, 6, 18

C

California, xiii, xvii, 4, 11, 12, 108, 114

D

Daughter. *See* Austin, Ruth
Divorce, 8, 11, 18, 100, 101, 126
Dodge, Mabel, 23, 29, 91

E

Europe
  England, 12, 13, 21, 45, 85, 95, 118
  France, 12, 45, 86
  Italy, 12, 13, 25, 86

F

Father. *See* Hunter, George
Fatherhood, 64, 86
Feminism, xii, xv, xix, xxii, xxiv, xxvi, 17, 19, 24-28, 30, 31, 38, 54, 78, 79, 89, 90, 92, 96,98-107, 109-116, 118-119, 121-123, 126-128
Feminist, vii, viii, xi, xii, xiii, xiv, xv, xvi, xx, xxii, xxiii, xxiv, xxv, xxvi, 2, 4, 13, 16-17, 2331, 49-50, 54, 57-58. 77-79, 84-85, 89-90, 96-113, 115, 116, 118-123, 125-128
Flynn, Elizabeth Gurley, 23, 43

G

Garver, Elizabeth Jordan, 16, 58, 84, 114
Goldman, Emma, 15, 22, 23, 29, 43, 48, 91
Graham Hunter, Susanna, 2, 3, 5, 6, 8, 9, 18, 107, 126
Grenache Village, 23, 24, 29, 31, 33, 51, 91, 93, 95

H

Hunter, George, 2, 3, 4, 18
Hunter, Jennie, 2, 18
Hunter, Jim, 2, 4, 6, 18
Husband. *See* Austin, Stafford Wallace

I

Illinois, 2, 126

M

Military, viii, 37-38, 40, 42, 44-46, 53
Mother. *See* Graham Hunter, Susanna
Motherhood, 81, 83, 86, 89, 90, 101, 102, 104, 117, 126

N

New York City, vii, ix, xii, xiii, xxii, xxvi, 14, 15, 17, 19, 20, 29, 35, 36, 38, 39, 40, 41, 42,43, 47, 48, 51, 52, 53, 55, 56, 62, 64, 65, 67, 72, 73, 74, 84, 86, 87, 88, 91, 108, 119, 127

P

Proto-feminist, viii, xi, xii, xv, 98, 123
Proto-feminism, 19, 114, 128

S

Sister. *See* Hunter, Jennie

T

Trade Union, 45, 65, 91, 120

W

Women's Suffrage, 3, 13, 14, 33, 47, 49, 50, 53, 54, 59, 64, 67, 70, 72, 73, 76, 89, 92, 95, 98,99, 103, 104, 113, 116, 117, 123, 125, 127
Women's trade union, 97
World War One (First World War, WWI), xii, xiii, xiv, xvi, xvii, xxii, 14-20, 24, 31, 35, 36-58, 62, 66, 69, 78, 82-85, 102, 109, 114-119, 121, 123, 125, 126, 128

Austin, Mary Hunter works:

A

A Woman of Genius, xii, 17, 19, 23, 31, 57, 126

C

Cactus Thorn, xxv

E

Earth Horizon: An Autobiography, xii, xv, xxi, xxii, 2, 3, 6, 9, 14, 15, 17, 18, 19, 25, 30, 31,32, 56, 57, 93, 95, 96, 113, 125

N

No. 26. Jayne Street, xii, xiv, xvii, xxv, 14, 15, 57, 68, 73, 76, 85, 86, 87, 88, 89, 91, 93, 94,95, 96, 125, 126

O

One Hundred Miles on Horseback, xxv

S

"Sex Emancipation Through War", xii, xvi, 15, 22, 33, 34, 36, 57, 77, 80, 81, 125

T

The American Rhythm, Studies and Re-expressions of Amerindian Songs, 123

"The Conversion of Ah Lew Sing", 7

The Ford, xxi, xiv, xvi, xvii, xviii, xxv, 5, 11, 14, 19, 25, 57, 58, 59, 60, 62, 63, 64, 65, 66,70, 75, 76, 96, 125, 126, 127

The Land of Little Rain, XV, 11

The Man Jesus: Being a Brief Account of the Life and Teaching of the Prophet of Nazareth,19, 25

"The Mother of Felipe", 7

The Young Woman Citizen, xii, xiv, xvi, xvii, xxv, 14, 15, 23, 24, 50, 55, 56, 57, 68, 69, 70,71, 73, 75, 76, 77, 80, 81, 95, 109, 116, 118, 125

www.ingramcontent.com/pod-product-compliance
Lightning Source LLC
Chambersburg PA
CBHW050552300426
44112CB00013B/1878